All rights reserved.

Copyright © 2021 by Angel Gaudia

Contact : gaudiaedition@gmail.com

ISBN 978-1-7776437-2-0

No part of this publication may be reproduced, distributed or transmitted in any form or by any means without prior written permission.

Note: The author is providing this book and its contents on an "as is" basis and make no representations or warranties of any kind with respect to this book or its contents. The author disclaims all such representations and warranties, including but not limited to warranties of health care for a particular purpose. In addition, the author assumes no responsibility for errors, inaccuracies, omissions, or any other inconsistencies herein.

The content of this book is for informational purposes only and is not intended to diagnose, treat, cure, or prevent any condition or disease. The author makes no guarantees concerning the level of success you may experience by following the advice and strategies contained in this book, and you accept the risk that results will differ for each individual. The testimonials and examples provided in this book show exceptional results, which may not apply to the average reader, and are not intended to represent or guarantee that you will achieve the same or similar results.

CONTENTS

Introduction v

Golden secret #1	1
Golden secret #2	9
Golden secret #3	19
Golden secret #4	23
Golden secret #5	28
Golden secret #6	35
Golden secret #7	42
Golden secret #8	45
Golden secret #9	49
Golden secret #10	54
Golden secret #11	57
Golden secret # 12	63
Golden secret #13	67
Golden secret #14	70
Golden secret #15	73
Golden secret #16	75
Golden secret #17	78
Golden secret #18	81
Golden secret #19	85
Golden secret #20	88
Golden secret #21	90
Golden secret #22	94
Golden secret #23	97
Golden secret #24	100
Golden secret #25	103
Golden secret #26	106
Golden secret #27	109
Golden secret #28	112
Golden secret #29	114

Golden secret #30	117
Golden secret #31	121
Golden secret #32	124
Golden secret #33	127
Golden secret #34	131
Golden secret #35	134
Golden secret #36	137
Golden secret #37	140
Golden secret #38	142
Golden secret #39	146
Golden secret #40	149
Golden secret #41	151
Golden secret #42	153
Golden secret #43	156
Golden secret #44	159
Golden secret #45	162
Golden secret #46	165
Golden secret #47	168
Golden secret #48	170
Golden secret #49	173
Golden secret #50	175
Golden secret #51	178
Golden secret #52	181
Golden secret #53	184
Golden secret #54	187
Golden secret #55	190
Golden secret #56	193
Golden secret #57	196
Golden secret #58	199
Golden secret #59	201
Golden secret #60	203
Golden secret #61	206
Golden secret #62	211
Golden secret #63	214
Golden secret #64	216
Golden secret #65	219

Golden secret #66	222
Golden secret #67	225
Golden secret #68	228
Golden secret #69	231
Afterword	233

INTRODUCTION

All our lives we seek happiness.

So, we work on all the exterior elements we can think of to make our lives better. But sometimes no matter what we do and no matter how much we work, we don't reach a point where we are truly happy with ourselves or with our lives. Even if we reach our dreams and goals we've been working on for years, we still can't seem to find true happiness. We are still not satisfied. We still feel a void deep inside. We may have everything we wished for, but we still feel empty and sad.

But why? Why does this happen? Why doesn't having the love relationship you always desired make you happy? Why doesn't having financial freedom you worked for all your life make you happy? Why doesn't working that dream job you studied several years for make you happy? Why don't travelling to the best places, buying amazing clothes, eating the best food, living in your dream house, or having your dream car make you feel happier either? Even with all these accomplishments, why are you unfulfilled and unsatisfied all the time?

We are so self-absorbed that we don't take the time to reflect on why this happens to us. And we wake up one day with deep internal injuries without knowing where they came from or why we feel so much pain. We don't know why, no matter what we do, we are still not *happy*.

We put so much time and energy—days and nights—into creating for ourselves a perfect life by acquiring money, love, and success, but we simultaneously neglect our own selves at the deepest level. And *that* is why we are not happy.

We neglect and harm ourselves without even realizing it. We do that until we become deeply hurt—until we figuratively kill our own *selves* with our own hands. We wake up one day and discover that life has no taste anymore, even with all that we've earned and all that we have. We don't even *see* it anymore. We don't see our blessings anymore. And, as always, we feel we are lacking something to be happy. So, we keep on trying to improve our exterior lives while thinking that will fix our sadness.

We keep on like that, trying to find a new love partner, new friends, new clothes, new places to go, or new activities to do—maybe changing career or house—and the list goes on! Time passes, and the pain in our hearts grows until we completely lose ourselves and no matter what we do, we can't find that happiness *any*where anymore.

We are not aware on a deep level that real happiness comes from *us*—from deep inside us. *We* are the ones who create it. And you know what? It is free; it is available and easy for each human being to possess: *the never ending fountain of true happiness.*

Believe it or not, we have access to an unlimited source of true happiness that is infinite like the universe. We have it *inside* of us. But we don't see it. And though some people know about it, they don't know how to unlock it even though it's the easiest thing to do.

Now, you may be asking: What is the real secret to being genuinely happy and living my best life?

Here is the answer: *To be genuinely, infinitely happy and have the best life, you need to be the best version of yourself because your life is a reflection of yourself on all levels.*

You may ask: What do I need to be the best version of myself?

The one and only ingredient you need is: SELF-LOVE.

Yes. *That* is the key to unlock true happiness, to create the best version of yourself, to become self empowered and to live your best life ever. Without it, you can't succeed in anything, even if you possess everything you desire.

With self-love, you can be truly happy even if you don't possess anything. This is the key ingredient that will create a powerful *you*. It will give you hope, motivation, drive, and determination to reach internal *and* external success at all levels in your life.

Note: *Self-love is not narcissistic or selfish. Only bad things come from narcissism and selfish behaviour. Real self-love is a healthy love that you have for your own self. And only good things come from this type of love.*

Do you know what will happen when you will start genuinely loving yourself? You will become a *high-value person*.

Why you should be a high-value person?

Well here is why: Because *everything* you attract in life will have the same value as you. Like attracts like.

Answer these questions: What are the things everyone want to possess? Who are the people we are all inspired by and dream to have in our lives?

We all want to possess things that have high value. And we all follow and love and hope to have high-value people in our lives.

I ask you a personal question, and you can take a minute here to think about your answer: Do you know your actual value? Do you know your actual *worth*?

If not, it is because you are so self-absorbed that you are unaware of it. And this may be the reason for your biggest pains today, the ultimate thing that is holding you back from reaching inner happiness and succeeding in everything you do. This is why you keep attracting low-value things, situations, and people in your life.

By reading this book, you will learn how to be aware of your value, how to evaluate it, and how to raise it so high it reaches the sky! You are the only one who can determine your value. No one on planet Earth has the power to do that except you. You build your value, and you can destroy it, too. You decide to put it at a certain level. You increase and decrease it. Your value is not the money in your bank account, your beauty, your intelligence, or your possessions. Your value is your self-worth. And your self-worth is measured by your self-love. The more you love yourself, the higher your worth will be, and the less you love yourself, the lower your worth will be.

What will happen if your worth is high, if you are a high-value person? What will your relationships look like? Who will you attract in your life? What will your self-confidence and everything you do in life be like? The answer is that you will attract high-value things, situations, and people in your life. You will attract value that matches yours.

So, what will happen if you have low value, if you have a low self-worth? Think about it. Maybe you are realising a lot of things at this very moment.

As a high-value person, you know exactly what you want from life and you are unafraid to advocate for yourself to achieve it. You never ever settle for less than what you deserve. Your self-confidence and your self-esteem are so powerful that you become a magnet for success at all levels.

This also means that you never let anyone hurt you, use you, or manipulate you ever again. You never burn yourself out in draining, no-value jobs, relationships, or life choices. Never *ever*!

Be aware here that it doesn't mean that you will not face hard situations and that life will become perfect. You need difficult situations and challenges to be able to learn, to grow and evolve.

When you genuinely love yourself, you think and act in ways that will fulfil that love. You want to satisfy that love and make it grow. All your conscious and subconscious actions focus on that vital goal: your own love need fulfilment. The happy news is that you don't need money, experience, friends, a lover, or anything. The only tools you need are your heart, your mind, your body, and your soul. And you can start right here, right now!

To understand self-love on a deeper level, think about a genuine love you have for someone in your life. It may be a lover, a friend, a sibling, a parent, or a child—it doesn't matter as long as you felt a powerful love and a deep connection with this person. How did you feel and act toward that person you loved so much? You:

- Care for that person.
- Feel protective over that person.
- Give affection and attention to that person.
- Support and motivate that person in their dreams and ambitions.
- Nurture that person.
- Want that person to grow and succeed in everything they do.
- Create memorable moments with that person.
- Make that person feel special and worthy.
- Care for that person's health and wellbeing.

- Want that person to be happy, and you do everything in your power to make that happen.

Of course, the list goes on; you yourself can add all the things you feel for the person or the people you genuinely love.

Now you see all that's mentioned here: those all are things that you feel and do for your own self when you have healthy and genuine self-love. And it's even more—it's deeper than that. It's a powerful connection with your own mind, body, and soul.

When you give and receive love, you naturally fulfil a love need. Because we *all* need to love and be loved. Either you give and receive it from others or your own self. The result is the same. You are fulfilling yourself. In that there is satisfaction, and it leads to true happiness.

Now, of course you need love from others. You are not in this world to live alone. Humans are created to bond and have relationships. But when you start loving yourself genuinely you will attract only good quality love from others. Because, once again, like attracts like.

When you fulfil a love need you feel happy and satisfied, you are motivated and confident, and you succeed at everything you do. You see life through the glasses of love no matter what your situation is.

No matter what, you will always be happy because you will always feel loved, even if you are not in a romantic relationship nor have an exterior source of love. You will have the essential love that can let you live your best life: this is the love for *yourself*. It is self-love that fulfils you and makes you happy at all levels. *This is the real success. Everything else is an <u>addition</u> to that happiness.*

This is *your* ultimate success. It is your main goal in life: to love yourself genuinely.

In this book, there are 69 golden secrets that will empower you and help you unlock the best version of yourself, live your best life, and succeed in everything you do to reach *real* happiness.

If you already know some of the golden rules, let this be a reminder for you! Human beings tend to forget, so the more we are reminded, the more we create awareness and we are pushed to do *actions to improve and see positive changes.*

And here is a secret before you even start reading: Repetition is key. The more you repeat your thoughts and actions, the more you will make your goals and dreams happen. So, if you feel consumed by your life and you feel lost, repeat reading this guide over and over again to remind yourself and never lose track of your goal to become the best version of yourself. If you get self-absorbed in your daily routine and your responsibilities, try to read a small part of these words once in a while—even for just fifteen minutes.

You'll also notice that the *repetition* technique is used in this book. Some information is repeated several times to make the most important parts *imprint* on your conscious and subconscious mind.

All the golden secrets are related one another, and you need them all working together to really unleash the magic and see a big impact and change in your life. Even if you may not see the connection, they are all related to your self-love and self-value. Be assured that applying the golden rules will have a *direct* impact on increasing your self-love and self-value.

Now, each one of us is at a certain level of awareness and each of us has her own capacity for change. Keep in mind that everything is a process. You need to work on yourself like this is your biggest and most important project in order to achieve results. It will take time, perseverance, and energy. But it will be your best investment and your greatest achievement in life.

Throughout this book you will be invited to evaluate and meditate on your life in order to be able to know your *self*, what you really want, and where you stand at all levels. Included are some specific questions to answer in the form of exercises.

Take a moment for yourself alone. Make yourself a good coffee or tea and grab a piece of paper. Take the time to answer to the questions by writing out your answers. That way, you will be able to see with your own eyes what is coming out of your mind. This is a very powerful technique from which you will benefit a lot. By reading your own answers, you will illuminate a lot of things about yourself and your life. You will better see your pitfalls and those things you should work on to improve yourself.

With the help of this book and your own effort and work, you will become empowered and self-aware. You will learn, you will heal, you will grow, and—most important of all—you will become the best version of yourself!

Let's start this adventure!

GOLDEN SECRET #1

From this moment on, from this exact *second*, everything you lived is in the past…

I want you to start right now to live the life that you deserve and to shape yourself into the best version of yourself. No matter what happened to you in the past, I want you to put that aside now and open your heart, your mind, and your soul for a new you. I want you to create the best version of yourself.

Our past has built us. It made us who we are today: the good and the bad of it. All the experiences, all the things we lived built and shaped us into the amazing person we are today. I want you to be proud of yourself. With all what happened to you, you are still standing, and still fighting, and still working for yourself. And if you choose to read this book, you are even more extraordinary because you still want and pursue the dream of becoming a better person no matter what happened to you in the past.

Of course, we gain success over the time, but we also carry burdens, losses, and deep emotional and possibly physical pain from hard-learned experience and trauma.

Sometimes you may feel like you are the only person on Earth who suffers from something happening to you. But each one of us is going through or has gone through a battle that no one else knows about. Each one of us is struggling with something that may have happened to us in our pasts or may be happening to us right now. We are all human beings, and we all have our pains and difficult moments. Life is not easy nor perfect for any one of us. You are not alone in this battle called *life*. I want you to take a deep breath and release it. If you need to, cry the pain you have deep down within your heart that no one knows about except you.

Take a moment.

You may cry at night over something that still hurts you. Maybe it's something from your childhood; maybe it was an accident; maybe you were physically or mentally abused; maybe you lost someone you cherished; maybe you were betrayed; maybe you were bullied about your physical image or upbringing or education by your friends, partner or even your own parents and family; maybe you lost your health, your job, your home, your friends, your family. Or maybe you are in a good place today but you are still carrying bad memories that are bringing you daily negative thoughts and painful emotions.

I know it's hard; it's destroying you from the inside out. No one in the world feels *your* pain the way you do. But right now, no matter what happened to you, I want you to be proud of yourself for surviving that.

Even if you know that it's in the past, you can't get rid of the emotions that you still carry today. You say to yourself "It's gone," but it still affects you. You preoccupy yourself and work on yourself, but it's hard. And you keep falling over and over. It's still there, haunting you. Even if you're lucky enough to forget for a while, it comes back and unfortunately the pain comes back with it.

Focusing on your past and what happened to you will only keep you self-absorbed. You will be forever stuck in that place: the past. While you are living in: today.

Is there a solution? you ask. How can I be completely healed from my heavy past that is still affecting me today? How do I move on? And how do I forget?

Well, first, you must acknowledge that *you can't change things*. It is what it is. What you lost, you may never find again. And what you lived can never be changed.

But today—at this precise moment—you have a precious thing: *yourself.* If you are still here and alive, no matter what state you are in today, then that's the most important thing. It's the best news ever! If you are alive, breathing and you have the mental capacity to read and understand this book right now, if what happened to you did not killed you and you are still among the human beings on planet earth, then you are more blessed then you think you are.

Here is a secret ; What doesn't kill you makes you stronger!

Now, you may never forget completely, and you may not be able to change what happened to you. We can't change the past, and you know that. But even if you can't change the past, *you have total control to change your present and your future.*

To begin your healing, you must shift the focus from your past and put it entirely on the *now*, the present, the immediate of and in your life.

You are a stronger person today than you were before, so you must use that power to shape the life you have always desired. Use your strength to positively shape yourself into the person you have always wanted to become. Don't let your bad past hold you back from that.

Living in the past and remembering it every day will only sabotage you on all levels, which is *not* what you want. You want to be happy, successful, and powerful. You want to shine, enjoy life, love, and feel loved. You want the best that life has to offer you. When you reach that place, the past will be something that you don't even remember.

No matter your age, if you are still alive, you want today to be beautiful. I ask you a question: Does yesterday even matter to you today? No. You are living right now at this moment, and you are reading these words. You want these moments to be amazing and the ones coming to be even better. So even if you believe you lost your youth and your precious years, then say this to yourself: "I am living *today*, and I want today to be the best day of my life!"

Life is a journey, and what happens to us happens for a reason. You may cry and question yourself every time: Why me? Why did this thing happen to me? Did I deserve that?

Have you analyzed about why it really happened? Did you ask yourself if this bad thing led you to a better place? Maybe you are stronger and a more mature person because of it, or maybe you are in a better situation today because of that past bad event. If it didn't lead you to a good place, it surely taught you something, and you gained experience and knowledge. And that experience and knowledge will feed you in a positive way for your present and future life.

The most important thing now is to refuse to accept that your past will hold you back from what you desire the most. You have to take an action right now and avoid letting it have control over you and *only you can do that.* Without anyone else's help (except yourself), you can *act* because you are the only one who has 100% control over your own feelings, mind, and soul.

I want you to order yourself right now to move on. Talk to yourself as if you were speaking to a child.

I want you to say this affirmation: "(say your own name), I order you right know to stop letting your past hold you back from the good things in life. I want you to stop crying over the bad things that happened to you. You are strong and *alive*, and you have the chance to make everything better. Free yourself from the heavy past and start living *now* because your present and future will be amazing!"

EXERCISE

1. Write down something that happened to you in the past that you still carry deep in your heart and that still affects you today.
2. Think; why does this thing still have power over your feelings?
3. Did you have the power to stop it from happening?
4. What emotions does this thing trigger in your mind? Name them.
5. Is there something that would help you move on and forget it forever?
6. If it's a person, are you seeking revenge?
7. What do you want to do to that person in order to get revenge?
8. Imagine yourself getting revenge. Now answer honestly: would you feel happier?
9. Would you be able to move on after that and forget what happened to you?

Now read what you wrote.

Feel free to express your feelings. If you want to cry or think about it, then do it.

Take a moment.

Now, take this sheet and cut it into as many pieces as possible. Say your goodbyes. Throw it into the toilet and flush it.

You will never see it again, which is exactly what you are going to do with the negative feelings you have about this ugly past experience and pain. Throw them in the toilet, say your goodbyes, and flush!

GOLDEN SECRET #2

At every level, you have things about yourself or in your life that you don't like. (We all do.) Things you wish you didn't have, situations you wish you never lived, or maybe people you wish you never met. Maybe it's in the past; maybe it's in the present. Maybe you are living something that is a result of a decision you made in the past, and you are stuck with it and can't change the result (or it's very hard to do so). Maybe you're suffering because of something you're born with, for example: a disease, or from a situation where you had no power to choose for yourself.

I ask you a question: can you change your height, the colour of your eyes, your skin type, your hair type, your origin, your family name, your blood type, or the day and time you were born?

Think about it for a minute. *Do you have the power to change those things?*

The answer is NO. You will never be able to change those things. You have to live with them; they are a part of you as long as you live, so either they're good or bad. If you don't like nor accept them, what will happen?

You will focus negatively on them, and it will create a complex within you. It will kill your self-esteem and self-confidence. You may even start hating yourself for them. You won't see all the good things you have and will only focus on that small percentage of things you don't like about yourself until they seem to become the biggest part of the cake! Then, everything in general will become negative for you because you put all your focus on it.

BODY IMAGE

Almost every human being have body image issues, no matter how beautiful and perfect a person can be, he or she can still suffer from body image issues, and that is a killer for self-confidence, self-worth, self-image and self-value. You may see a person who seems perfect to you but when you talk to him or her, he or she complains about one little thing (such as his or her body type for example). That person obsesses over that until she can't see herself beautifully at all and start believing that it's a handicap. You may have seen that pattern with a friend or a celebrity, someone you know casually, or even in yourself.

Now, as I said, there are things we can't change. We are born this way. Your skin type for example: you can't change that. There are many other things as well. So, if the things you don't like about your body are never going to change, what does that mean for you? Will you be sad forever? Will you hate yourself? Or, even worse, will you punish yourself by telling yourself that you are worthless and without value?

What is there to do about the things you don't like about yourself? Remember: this doesn't only apply to your physical features; it applies *to everything* in you and your life.

Here is a question I want you to ask to yourself when you hate something in your life or about yourself: Do I have the power to change that thing?

If your answer is *no*—if you don't have power to change it— then the thing you have to do about it is: *accept it*.

You must learn to *accept* the things within you over which you have no power to change: the things you were born with or that were there when you came to this life, or that happened in your past and you can't erase anymore. Those things are there and will live with you forever.

Acknowledge that you did not create yourself. You lack power to change everything. Instead, you must *accept*.

Do you know what *real* acceptance is?

It's not saying to yourself, "Pfffff... Okay, it is what it is. I can't change those things, so I will live with them." No.

To truly accept something, you must own it and be genuinely grateful for it.

Here is the secret to real acceptance. Here is how you change a thing you don't like about yourself, making something negative become positive: you accept it by being grateful for it. You must be grateful even (especially!) if it's something you don't like. I know it is a complex concept, and it may be difficult to comprehend. But the moment you are grateful for the things you don't like and can't change is the moment that your perception of yourself and your life will be changed forever. And even more than that, do you know what will happen? The things you do not like will vanish; they will completely disappear from your mind. You will not notice them ever again because they won't matter anymore. Suddenly, you will be proud of them and you will radiate with self-confidence !

Accept, cherish, and love the things you can't change about yourself and your life. *Make them your best assets, those things that make you special and unique.* If they are that bad, then you can turn them into a motivation. They can be a great source of power for you. And know that they are like they are because *they are meant to be so*. Maybe one day you'll know why, and you'll be grateful.

You will feel so light and at peace inside when you acknowledge the fact that it is what it is. You can't change it, but if you accept it and are grateful for it, then it will be an illumination and a liberation for your mind and soul.

Certainly, you've heard about Cleopatra, the queen of ancient Egypt, one of the most well-known and powerful queens in human history. If you search for her on the internet, you will find numerous articles saying that she was one of the most beautiful women in the world. She conquered the hearts of the most powerful kings of that time, Julius Caesar and Marc Antony. Without detailing her entire life, we are just going to take inspiration from how she dealt with her body image issues and insecurities. Even if everyone says she was one of the most beautiful women in the world, she was still a woman and a human being, and, like each one of us, she had her own insecurities.

Even today we hear about Cleopatra's beauty secrets. She is still an icon. But here, I will tell you one truth. It was not her beauty secrets that made her beautiful. In fact, did you know that Cleopatra has been described by many painters and historians as being physically ugly!

Yes, you read that right. Maybe you already know about Cleopatra before I tell you about her, and in your mind she was a woman who embodies mystical and extraordinary beauty. But, she was in fact *not* a physically beautiful woman. There are some sculptures and drawings of her face where you can see that she was not as physically appealing as everyone thought she was. Have a look on the internet about this whole topic describing Cleopatra. Historians have said that she did not have beautiful facial features nor a perfect body, and most of the women around her were more beautiful than she.

Isn't that crazy?

What was the secret behind Cleopatra's mystery if not her beauty? How was she able to be called the most beautiful woman in the world if she was not beautiful to the human eye? And how did she attract the most powerful kings of the time when there were plenty of other women more beautiful than she was? How did she get them to marry her? No, it is not because she was a queen. Because, in fact, it was her husband Julius Caesar who made her queen of Egypt. He could have taken the throne and killed her right away, but he made her his wife and his queen.

Note: one of the most talked-about things in describing Cleopatra as not beautiful was and is her big, masculine nose. She lived with it all her life and never went to a plastic surgeon to change it, and yet she still was considered the most beautiful woman in the world. What were her beauty secrets if at that time there were no fillers, no botox, no aesthetic procedures to allow her to change her facial attributes? She had to live with that big nose *forever*.

How come a not-so-physically-attractive woman like Cleopatra was able to conquer two of the most powerful men in human history and be the beauty icon that everyone one was and is mesmerized by all the way up until today?

What is her *real* beauty secret?

Want to know the answer?

Here it is: *acceptance.*

Cleopatra accepted herself; she accepted her imperfections and made them her best assets. She did not cry over poor body image nor insecurities. She did not focus on the "negative" things she possessed but rather on the positive ones. She worked on being the best version of herself that she could instead of focusing negatively on her big nose! She knew she couldn't change her nose. And she also knew that her nose didn't define her. It wasn't something that would make her ugly or unattractive. She refrained from comparing herself to other women who were more conventionally beautiful. She saw herself beautiful as she was. She was *proud* of who she was. She owned and valued herself. Raw confidence radiated from her. *That's* what made her shine like no one else.

Would Cleopatra have been able to attract two men who ruled the world if she had been insecure? Even if she had been physically perfect, would she have had access to everything and everyone? Nope.

Cleopatra valorised herself. She saw the value that she herself brought to the table. She was confident and sure that she was the hottest woman out there. She didn't bring any other woman down to appear magnificent. No, she stayed focused on improving what she was able to improve about *herself*. She became the best version of herself because she had self-love.

She was genuinely grateful for her physique. She believed in herself. She loved herself for who she was and with what was naturally given to her. She did not focus on the things she couldn't change. She improved things she knew she had the power to change: her personality, culture, and knowledge. She improved her state of mind, hygiene, charisma, hair, smell, artistic skills, her body's health, and so on.

The queen of Egypt was so charming, confident, charismatic, respectful, polite, powerful in communications—everything that came out of her mouth was beautiful—that *everyone* in her time period saw only beauty coming from her at every level. Can you believe all that with a huge, masculine, unflattering nose? She was a shining star. Historians have said that everyone who met her fell immediately under her charm. She was hypnotizing, and no one could resist her.

She had a confidence of a *queen*. And the secret behind her true self-love and self-esteem? Acceptance and gratitude!

All this starts with a decision. The day you decide to accept every facet of yourself will be the day that begins a new you. The *best* you.

Now, I want to you to do this next exercise honestly. Don't be shy about the things you don't like about yourself and your life; write them down. They are only for you to read. If Cleopatra did this exercise, she might write of her nose or her not-so-beautiful facial features. Write the things that *you* **cannot** change about yourself. Then, write the things you don't like about yourself and your life that you ***can*** change.

Read your answers and view everything you wrote as a blessing instead of a curse. I want you to focus on each thing you wrote and feel real *acceptance* for every single one. Think about how you will feel at the end of this exercise. You may have a rush of emotion and start crying because the feeling is powerful and overwhelming. That's okay! Express yourself. *Relieve* yourself.

EXERCISE

1. Name five or more things about your physical appearance that you have never liked and that you cannot change.
2. Name five or more things about your physical appearance that you have never liked but that you *can* change.
3. Name five things about your personality that you don't like but know you can change.
4. Name five things in your life that you don't accept and you cannot change.
5. Name five things in your life that you don't accept but you *can* change.

GOLDEN SECRET #3

WE ALWAYS HEAR ABOUT IT: GRATITUDE.

But what *is* gratitude?

Gratitude means being thankful and genuinely appreciate and love something you have or that was given to you.

A genuinely grateful person is not only being thankful for the good things in her life but also for the bad things. Having a grateful mindset will lead you to real happiness, self-confidence, self-love, self-worth, self-value, self-esteem, abundance, success, love, and every possible good thing you can possess for yourself or in this life.

Being grateful is not something you say just with your mouth. "Oh, I am grateful for my life and everything I have." No, you don't just say it. You must *feel* it. To know if you are truly grateful here is something to notice and remember: you become overwhelmed. You feel a powerful energy and emotion in your whole body, in your bones, and you even get tears in your eyes.

Make a test of it. Ask people around you to see if they are grateful for something and analyse their answers. If they are truly grateful you will feel it, but if they are not you will only hear it. When a person is truly grateful, she feels it deeply in her heart, and you will see her eyes sparkle and her face glow, and she may become overwhelmed.

Gratitude is a feeling. It's more than appreciation and thankfulness.

GRATITUDE IS THE TRUE FORM OF LOVE.

And because it's true love, it will bring you all the feelings you experience with love.

The magic here is that the more grateful you are, the more you will attract good things in your life. The more grateful you are, the more you will be happy and satisfied with what you have, and you'll have even more good things to be grateful for.

You will shine and feel so peaceful because you are present each second of your life, even in bad moments. Just by being grateful for *everything*, you actually create for yourself a positive mindset! It's a kind of gift from your gratitude.

Some people say, "How can I be grateful about something bad that happened to me?" Well, firstly, there is always something even worse that could have happened to you—just look around you. You may find someone struggling with the same thing as you, but their case is a lot worse, and you wonder if you could bear the situation the other person is in. There is *always* someone who is suffering more than you—*always*.

If you lost a finger, someone out there lost a hand. If you lost a hand, someone out there lost an arm. If you lost an arm, someone out there lost both their arms! And it goes on.

There is always someone who is worse off than you. If what you are going through is horrible and unbearable, I have sincere empathy for you. But always be grateful it is not worse. Because, believe me, it can be! If you are going through hardship, *keep going.*

Secondly, you never know if that bad thing or situation could lead you to something very great you thought you could never have. You have experienced this throughout your life: a bad thing came to you, but it somehow eventually transported you to something great, all without even realizing it.

There is a lesson to be learned about gratitude. When you are grateful, you will attract positive things to be grateful for. Likewise, when you are ungrateful, you will attract negative things to be ungrateful for.

Always be grateful—for the good *and* the bad!

EXERCISE

1. Name ten positive things for which you are grateful.
2. Name ten negative things about yourself or in your life that you *could* be grateful for (but you aren't).
3. Write more about five things you are not grateful for by complaining about them. Here's the catch: write after each one how that thing could actually be worse.

Now, take a little time to imagine if the things you are grateful for were taken from you. How would your life change for the worse?

GOLDEN SECRET #4

How well do you know yourself?

1. Not at all.
2. A decent amount.
3. Very well.

Congratulations. With this answer, you know how much power you have over yourself!

There is a rule that says: *Knowledge is power, and with power you can control everything.*

The better you know yourself, the better you can control yourself. The more you know yourself, the more you can make the right choices and do things that satisfy and fulfil yourself. The reverse is also true. If you *don't* know yourself, you lose power over yourself, and you let everything and everyone else have control over you instead.

You must know who you are on a deep level. This is the very first step in the process. Without knowing yourself, you can't improve yourself. How can we improve something we don't know anything about?

Ask yourself questions in order to know the *why*; find the *why* within everything in your life. The *why* will lead you to correct information about who you are. When you do this, be honest to yourself. Don't be shy if you see your weaknesses coming out in the process. No one is going to judge. You will work on those weaknesses to build your inner strength.

Become a detective and spy yourself so that you will have as much information as possible about you. Ask your own questions, and look into your deepest self to find your answers.

Your questions can look like these:

- How do I mentally behave in bad situations?
- How do I react to good and bad things happening to me?
- What do I truly like?
- What triggers me?
- What makes me angry?

- What makes me happy?
- Where do I find comfort?
- What motivates me?
- What are my habits?
- What are my limits?
- What breaks my heart?
- What are my skills, ambitions, beliefs, and goals?
- What are the mission and purpose of my life?
- What do I want the rest of my life to look like?
- What kind of people do I want to surround myself with?

Ask yourself these questions and any others that you can think of on a regular basis. Write them in a journal, or simply meditate on them. Discover your answers and find the *why* of each answer. This is how you will learn a lot about yourself.

Knowing yourself may not be easy, it's true, but it's worth it in the end. Reflect on what you know about yourself. Perhaps take a personality test like the Myers-Briggs Type Indicator to learn more about how you express your thoughts and emotions and react to everything and everyone around you. Think about why you do what you do. When you're happy, ask yourself why you're happy. Similarly, when you're angry or sad, take a step back and ask yourself *why*. When you know why, you can adjust to your surroundings and act in your own best interest more easily. Think about your core values; what are they? Have they changed from when you were younger? What's remained the same? Similarly, who are you when no one else is looking?

Think about several times in your life when you felt a sense of accomplishment, joy, or peace. Now think about the times that have caused the most pain or embarrassment. What are the differences between them? How does each memory reinforce or conflict with your core values? Where do you look for happiness and how do you avoid pain?

Think about the relationships you have with other people: your friends, coworkers, and family. Which of these relationships feel easy? Which ones feel difficult? Can you figure out why? Remember, the key is *why*. Introspective reflection will lead you in the right direction, so take time to learn more about yourself and you will have more power over yourself as well!

You constantly evolve, grow, and change, and so does everything inside your mind. It's important to know acknowledge these changes and accept the new thing or behaviour that appears inside you at each crucial junction of your life. Never lose track of yourself; learn and be aware of your own evolution so you will always have the best knowledge about yourself.

Finally, always keep in mind that the more you know yourself, the more you have control over yourself and your life. It's only through knowing your deep, raw and real self that you will upgrade, level up, change and be a better version of you.

GOLDEN SECRET #5

Do you want a change in one or several areas of your life? A major, positive change that will make you evolve?

If you're reading this book, your answer is probably *yes*.

Do you believe your potential changes will only happen when the situation progresses naturally by itself or when you have some kind of exterior motivation?

For example, you think to yourself, "I'll start eating healthy when I have less work," or "I'll start eating healthy three months before summer so I can have a beautiful body."

Do you think like that? If yes, then read this carefully:

The changes that you are waiting for will never happen if you don't take responsibility for yourself and move toward them.

You are the one and only person completely in charge of yourself at all levels.

And you will read this over and over everywhere in this book.

We have this sad belief that most of the time we have to rely on others to help us achieve our dreams, emotional stability, happiness, love, or anything else—material or otherwise.

For example, do you have a belief that your life partner will provide everything you need? Will that person provide you happiness, love, care, maybe money, and stability for the rest of your life?

Were you hoping that your situation would change because someone comes and sweeps you off your feet? Were you hoping that someone would save you or something would happen and your situation would immediately get drastically better?

At some point in life, everyone has wished for the seemingly impossible: to have a magic wand and make everything magically happen as we desire.

"But, there is no magic wand," you say. "It doesn't exist."

Incorrect! Magic wands *do* exist, and they can make things happen for you!

Even more than that, you have a magic wand with you *right now*. The magic you have always wanted is in your possession as you read these words.

The magic wand is you!

You are the magic wand that will change everything in your life and that will bring you your heart's desire. *You* are the magic wand that will turn everything bad in your life into good. *You* are the miracle and the real change in your own life.

Answer these questions, and you will see how that is possible, even if you don't believe it:

- Who thinks inside your head?
- Who speaks with your mouth?
- Who sees with your eyes?
- Who controls your body?
- Who controls your mind and thoughts?
- Who controls your heart and emotions?
- Who controls your actions?

If your answers are: *me*, then you've got your proof!

You are the only one who has *complete* control over yourself. No other human being on this earth has control over you but you.

I want you to say this out loud right now: "I am fully in control of myself. No human being on this earth has control or power over me except me. I totally control my mind, my body, and my soul."

You can choose who you are because there is no one who knows you better than you know yourself. You decide on everything that touches you at every level.

This is called *power*! It's the best magic power you can possess.

If you discover that you have *no* control over yourself, it may be because of a negative person or situation. This means that you are in a toxic relationship or an otherwise toxic environment where you were manipulated. Get your freedom back from this toxicity—you are the only human being who should have control over yourself. Remind yourself that you let yourself be manipulated, and you chose to stay in that toxic environment where you lost your most precious power. This may have happened for a multitude of reasons, but instead of focusing on why it happened, let's grow and let's see your liberation. You can free yourself the second you decide to free yourself. When you love yourself enough, you won't allow anyone or anything to cross your boundaries nor have emotional, physical, or even financial control over you.

Have you said the following to yourself or anyone else? "Well, I don't have a choice; it's not my fault. I don't control things; it's not in my power."

We have *all* been there. Sometimes, we blame what happens to us on others or on the situation, and when we're in a bad place, we tend to think it's because we don't have control over things nor over what happened. The problem with this is that even if you don't say it you may still actually *believe it*. That's bad. If you have reached a point where you believe that you have no control over yourself and over what is happening to you, then you need to stop right now and realize that this is simply not true.

This type of thinking is called *victim mentality*.

Victim mentality is a psychological behaviour that you should absolutely be aware of in order to *avoid* it. If you always think your failures are because of something or someone else no matter the circumstance, then you have victim mentality. Victim mentality will never let you succeed at anything in life. You must be accountable for your successes *and* your failures. You must always blame yourself first because, as we said, you control *yourself*.

That doesn't mean that sometimes people and situations won't make your life hard or block you to reach your goals. But in most cases, you allow those people or situations to have an impact on you. You didn't fight enough, and you failed. In that moment, blame yourself because you did not control yourself instead of letting a person or situation control you such that you end up with victim mentality.

If you are at a stage where you truly believe that your failures are because of others, then you have reached a very low level of this kind of behaviour. Question yourself. Be honest with yourself on the real *why*. Why did you really fail in that thing?

At a certain point, you must take things in hand and save *yourself* to reach past that failure. Constantly question yourself, and you will find the truth in your own answers. You will see that you allowed people and situations to control you, and you ended up seeing yourself as a victim when really you yourself are to blame.

The beautiful thing in this is that you will become *self-aware*. Self-awareness is the ultimate key, and it comes by reflecting on the *why*. When you ask yourself questions and are honest with yourself, that is how you grow.

> You are 100% in control of your mind, body and soul.
> No one else does.

Please take a moment, and think about it. Whatever situation you are in, you *can* make a choice and make a change.

When you have control, you have the power to change everything, so stand up for yourself!

EXERCISE

1. Write three big changes you want to make to your physical appearance.
2. Write three changes you want to happen in your overall health.
3. Write three changes you want to happen in your career.
4. Write three changes you want to happen in your love life.
5. Write three changes you want to happen in your relationships.
6. Write three other changes you want to happen in your overall life.

GOLDEN SECRET #6

WE ARE ALL IN A CONSTANT QUEST FOR HAPPINESS. Everything we do in life is based on finding happiness. Even if we are not consciously aware of this, it's the object of our deepest desires.

The source of happiness varies from one person to another because we each have our own standards and desires but our overall goal is the same: happiness.

From a young age we learned to believe that happiness is the fruit of something we earn by *doing* an action, *possessing* something, *living* a certain way, or *surrounding* ourselves with certain people. We think that by having the best job, an attractive partner, a big house, a trendy wardrobe, a luxurious car, a sexy body, and a perfect family we will experience eternal joy and happiness. Sometimes it can be by obtaining fame and notoriety or by being accepted by certain groups of people. In all cases, we work toward those elements for years if not all our life to obtain them believing the we will feel fulfilled and happy.

Happiness is a puzzle and a very personal thing. What makes *you* happy won't necessarily make someone else happy. It's a kind of fingerprint; its recipe is unique to each one of us, but the taste is the same for everyone.

Here's the truth about happiness:

Happiness is not found through exterior means like being with certain people or living in certain situations. Real happiness is found inside oneself. And at this very moment, you already have everything inside yourself to feel happy. You just have to unlock it.

Have you ever really wanted something so badly that you thought it was the key to everlasting happiness? Maybe it was a dream job, money, an educational diploma or degree, a perfect wedding, a dream car, or even meeting the love of your life. And finally, after waiting for so long and working so hard, you finally got what you really desired. Maybe it even took years to achieve, *years* during which you waited, prayed, wished, and dreamed it would be yours.

What happened after that?

After a while your excitement inevitably disappeared because this thing you wanted much became your new normal. In fact, this thing you dreamed about for months or years maybe brought you problems and headaches instead of giving you the good things you thought you would get from it.

That thing you wished for so long just did not give you the happiness you expected. Or it was temporary. So, now you're back at square one, feeling the void again.

Maybe you ask, how can a person who has no family, who lives in poverty, who has no job, no romantic relationship, no physical beauty be happy ? For example.

The answer is this: that person is *grateful*. You see how much gratitude is one of the most powerful things in this world. When we are grateful, we feel love and so we are happy. Even without possessing a single thing, if we are genuinely grateful, we will never lack for anything, and we will be happy. Everything that we acquire adds joy to our lives, but those things don't determine our happiness.

You have surely seen someone who is extremely poor—maybe it's in a *National Geographic* or a video on YouTube or TV and *you saw* that poor person was happy. You could see it in her face and eyes. And visa versa. I'm sure you have seen someone who is rich, fabulous, and famous who has everything he or she could possibly want, but that person was not happy.

The real source of genuine happiness is gratitude.

Now, here's the million-dollar question: how do I reach *real* happiness?

There is nothing that can and no one who can provide you eternal happiness. It comes from within, and everything and everyone after that only *add* to your happiness. When you rely on someone, a situation, or something to provide you happiness, you now know that it's temporary. You have no control over those things and people, and they can change, and once they change, your happiness will, too.

Real happiness can only be reached by building it yourself, inside yourself and for yourself. Your happiness should *never* depend or rely on anything or anyone else except yourself.

True happiness is a recipe, and you need several ingredients, including gratitude, acceptance, and a positive mindset. The most important ingredient is *love*, and not just any type of love. You need this specific type to start: *self-love*.

Human beings cannot live without love, and the first love bond you should have with a human is with yourself.

Self-love is not a narcissistic or selfish kind of love. It's the real love for and acceptance of yourself. It's the respect you have for your person, the care and nurturing you provide yourself. It doesn't have anything to do with anyone or anything else.

This type of love that you cultivate for yourself is something that you own completely. You control it. It's one of your most precious possessions along with your life and your time. No one in this world can take it away from you.

And this is why you can be always truly happy even if you don't have the things or the people you desire the most in your life.

The basic recipe for happiness is as follows:

Acceptance + Gratitude + Self-love

Let the good things, people, accomplishments, and acquisitions be a *completion*, an *addition* to this basic recipe. Think about the trio above like a yummy cake and everything else I just mentioned like the toppings. They add flavour to the cake, yes. But even without toppings, you still have a delicious cake.

You *are* a happy person. This is base. Everything around you that brings you happiness is an extra. With or without it, you are happy. If you start living this way, you will become *invincible*. Nothing bad will affect you anymore. No negativity will be able to touch your inner peace. Something might put you in a bad mood for a while, but It will never lead you to depression or self-destruction. Your happiness will be indestructible because you are the only one who has power and control over it.

EXERCISE

This exercise will help you meditate deeply on the source of your actual happiness.

1. Name five things in your life that make you genuinely happy at this moment.
2. If those things where taken away from you, would you be unhappy?

3. Name ten things that would make you happy if you acquired them.
4. Imagine never having those things. Would you be unhappy?

GOLDEN SECRET #7

You have at least one goal you want to achieve to make a significant change in your life. I know this because you are reading this book! Some goals are small and short term, and some of them are big and long term. Whatever the size, there are actions that you need to take to make positive change begin to happen.

Sometimes what happens is that you write down your goals and resolutions, but you never start working on them. Or maybe you start, but then life happens and you get off track.

There may be major factors delaying you: lack of motivation, life responsibilities, or fear of taking risks. Maybe you procrastinate because your goal feels like a pipe dream and you think you need magic to make it happen.

Whatever the cause, here is the result: you put it off and put it off. You delay until that change never happens at all!

If you are daydreaming about achieving your goals and changing your life, then the best time to start (or re-start) is **_NOW_**. Not in one month nor one year. Not when spring comes nor when you finally finish your bachelor's degree. Not when you think you'll have enough money nor when you move to another country nor when all the planets align. *Right now!*

STOP FINDING EXCUSES! THEY JUST DELAY THE GOODNESS THAT BELONGS IN YOUR LIFE!

You are losing time sitting at the crossroads just waiting to become your best self. You're betting that you will still have time to begin later. No, the time is *now*!

Your life is NOW, not the in the past and not in the future!

You know what will happen if you decide to start later? *Nothing* will happen, that's what; you'll never start in the first place! Worse than waiting for the perfect moment to start is when you begin to give yourself conditions for starting. Like beginning isn't already hard enough!

Start using the power of NOW right now !

It doesn't matter if you want to make major or minor changes in your life. Start *now* where you are with what you have. Let today be the starting point and one day soon be the finish line.

Make a teeny tiny step towards that change, but make it today. Don't wait for tomorrow because you will keep putting off, and you will end up losing time and waking up a year or a decade later regretting that you never started when you had the time and inclination to do so.

You never know what the future holds. You may have options today that you don't have tomorrow. So, let the change start NOW !

EXERCISE

1. Name ten big changes you want to happen in your life.
2. Name ten (or more) small changes you want to happen in your life.
3. Read them all and identify which ones you can start right now. (it should be all of them !)

GOLDEN SECRET #8

It's possible you may've lost precious things before this moment. Maybe you lost your time, health, mental health, youth, energy, opportunities, a dear one or something else you cherished about yourself or in your life that's now gone.

You feel great heartache because you're convinced that you will never get back what you lost—or even if you do get it back, it will never be the same. It's possible to feel completely destroyed by this idea. Plus, you may feel guilty because you think you may could have avoided the loss at the time. (Or maybe not! Maybe it was unexpected and sudden.)

Whatever the case, you blame yourself and the people who lead you there (if they are any involved) . You constantly replay the situation in your head, trying to figure out if you could've done anything differently and if that would have even mattered. You may feel regret and hopelessness for yourself and your future. At this very moment, you may be devastated and unable to go on. It dogs you mentally and emotionally.

You are right to feel that way. Loss is a heartbreaking thing to live. Maybe you were responsible for it, or maybe you weren't. Maybe you made bad choices, and now you suffer the results.

However, guilt, regret, pain, and tears will not give you back what you lost. And actually, you already know that.

Think about it this way: each day, each hour, each minute, each *second* is a chance for you to live fully and purposefully and live up to your potential. Even if you feel like you wasted your entire life up to this point, there's still hope: it's never too late. Whether you're 25 or 95, you can turn over a new leaf and start again *right now*. Want to be a master in a certain field? Well, the best time to start practicing was fifteen years ago, as you know! But the second-best time is now. Want to learn to paint or begin a completely new career? You *can*, but you have to *start now*. I'm not saying it's easy by any means, but it's *possible*. Everything is possible even if it's not rational or logical. And that is where the magic is. If you learn to believe that, you will unlock incredible doors that will lead you to places you never thought you can reach no matter what your mental, financial or physical state actually is.

In Japan, there's a type of craft called *Kintsugi* in which skilled artisans repair broken pottery with gold or silver. The cracks, then, become part of the story of the piece, and the pottery is all the more beautiful for having been broken. You, my friend, may be heartbroken at what you have lost or maybe at what could never be, but if you repair yourself you will also be more beautiful. Never forget that you are your own skilled artisan. You know yourself best than no one else.

Whatever situation you have lived through or are in now, whatever happened or is happening to you, if you are reading these words, you are here, you are alive, and *it's never too late*.

Remember, it doesn't matter how big your loss was nor what opportunity you may have missed; there is hope for you to rebuild, correct yourself and the situation, and change for good.

No matter your age and the time you lost, you still can jump on the train to the places you've always wanted to go. Again; it's *never* too late!

EXERCISE

1. Name three things you think it may be too late for you to have or do.
2. Name three opportunities you lost and about which you are still sad.
3. Name three things you wanted to do in life for which you think it's too late.

GOLDEN SECRET #9

We all hear about it—and we all want it! What is it? A positive mindset. You may have read books about it, read articles on the internet, or watched YouTube videos on how to cultivate it and increase it.

But what *is* a positive mindset?

A positive mindset is encouraging and nurturing positive thoughts in your mind.

It is that simple.

It is approaching life with an outlook that will return positivity to all areas of your life.

Positivity is light in the darkness.

It's easy to fall into darkness in life, so if you don't actively grow a strong positive mindset, you may easily be affected by negativity.

If you don't have a positive attitude towards life, you may handle situations poorly and react to everything with negativity. This, in turn, will cause you more negativity. It's a vicious circle.

Remember: having a positive mindset is *not* fighting against your negative thoughts and feelings to make them disappear. It is instead increasing your *positive* thoughts and feelings. People need negativity as a counterbalance.

A positive person is a person who thinks and feels positively most of the time and who can see the positive side of any negative situation. Because this person controls his or her thoughts and decide to have a positive outlook on life, he or she will make good decisions and this, in general, will bring him or her good results.

Being a positive person means that what you think and feel most of the time is positive. That's it. Because your actions are a reaction to your thoughts, your actions will be genuinely positive if your mindset is positive.

We attract what we think. And if we think negative thoughts, we will attract negative situations to our lives.

"But," you may say, "I am a super positive person, so why do I keep attracting negative things?"

Because it's meant to be. Bad things happen for a reason; despite what else you may think, there is purpose behind it. No one can live life without negative things happening *some*times. You need to learn, improve, and evolve. You need hard challenges to grow stronger. But here is what you can do with a positive mindset: you can attract more positive things to your life, *and* you can neutralize the negative things with positive thinking and a good attitude.

To cultivate a positive mindset, you must clean your thoughts and avoid negative feelings as much as possible while indulging positive ones. For example, if you think about getting revenge for something bad that happened to you ten years ago, your negative thoughts will cause even more negative thoughts and feelings. It will put you in a negative mental state, which will attract even more negativity inside your mind and your life.

Here are negative emotions you should be wary of:

Fear

Anger

Culpability

Sadness

Rage

Revenge

Replace them as much as possible with these positive emotions:

Love

Joy

Satisfaction

Contentment

Gratitude

Amusement

Happiness

Serenity

> If you imagine your thoughts on a scale. It's the only thing that should not be balanced in yourself and your life: the positive thoughts side must be "heavier"—so to speak—than the negative thoughts side.

Two things you can do to grow your positive mindset:

1. Meditate often.
2. Engage yourself as much as possible in things that help make you feel positive.
3. Surround yourself with positive people who uplift you.

The more you do things you like and things that give you positive emotions, the more you will get rid of negative emotions and thoughts.

Despite all this, you should not quest for a perfectly positive mind because negative emotions and thinking are vital. They give a solid counterpoint to positive emotions; without the negative you can't even know the positive. Don't focus on *eliminating* the negative thoughts completely but instead *increasing* positive ones.

Having a generally positive mindset is key for a happy and successful life, and with it you can be the best version of yourself and live your best life!

GOLDEN SECRET #10

YOUR ENVIRONMENT IS ONE OF THE MOST IMPORTANT THINGS that will help lead you to success in everything.

Can a jungle flower blossom in a desert? Can a wild sea fish live in a bathtub? Your environment is crucial in order for you to succeed, evolve, and be happy.

Your environment mainly includes the people who surround you, the place you live (the country or city), the society where you are, the house where you live, every exterior element to your mind and soul. And that even includes your body!

If you are living in a toxic environment because of toxic people, then distance yourself from them. If you don't feel happy in the house you are in and you can move, then move. If you feel you don't have opportunities to grow and have a better life in your actual hometown, then move if you can and start a new life elsewhere.

You must understand that sometimes you can't evolve in a bad environment.

And you may not be aware of this, but being in a bad environment can be the principal cause holding you back from success and happiness.

Create for yourself an environment where you will be able to succeed and live the life you have always desired.

To do this, start by evaluating your actual environment, including the:

- People in your life.
- Place where you call home.
- State of your body—it's the house of your mind.
- Country and society where you live.

What are some things that are not favourable to you that are holding you back from your desired goals in your actual environment? Change or improve them as much as you can, and you will see the immediate positive impact this will have on you. To do this you have to sometimes take risks. But if you don't take risks you may stay stuck forever where you are!

Take a moment and look around yourself right now. What do you see? Do you feel safe and secure where you are? Do you feel healthy mentally and physically? Is it the place where you can realize are your dreams? Think about the people with whom you surround yourself. Are they supporting you and helping you lead your best life? Or, are they bringing you down and creating a toxic atmosphere? Just ask yourself questions about your overall environment and analyze your answers. Maybe you will discover things you were not aware of that will illuminate you to make some changes.

Your environment is the unsung hero of many success stories. A good environment is crucial for your success. Are you giving yourself the surroundings you need not to just live but to *thrive*? Like a plant in good soil, you are a being who needs a good environment to grow.

GOLDEN SECRET #11

WE ARE HUMAN BEINGS, AND WE NEED SOCIAL INCLUSION. We were created to have relationships and bond with one another. It starts with your parents and siblings and moves to your neighbours and friends, and the list goes on. The people around you affect and influence your life directly and indirectly.

The closer the relationship you have with someone, the more you will be affected in a positive or negative way.

Did you know that the ten closest people to you are the ones who influence you the most? They influence you in everything: the way you talk, your taste, your life choices, the way you think, your moods, your personality, your lifestyle... just *everything*. They have *a huge* impact on you and your life at all levels.

It's really important to choose carefully the people you allow in your daily life. Your parents, siblings, and family may be an exception, but your life partner and close friends are the ones I am talking about here.

If you surround yourself with positive people who give you joy, motivation, and good vibes, then this will reflect positively onto you. And if you surround yourself with toxic and negative people, then this will also have an impact on you.

Do you want to become physically fit? Imagine what would happen if you surrounded yourself with friends who are all into fitness. They have healthy food routines, they go to the gym five days a week, most of their conversations are about how to stay fit, etc. What will happen to you if those are the people you interact with on a daily basis? *You will slowly become like them.* You will start to share the same thinking and goals.

Do you want to be financially well off? Insert yourself into a group of friends who are business entrepreneurs and multimillionaires. What will happen to you then? You will share their life habits, goals, and conversations. Learning from them, you will adopt the same lifestyle routines and end up becoming a multimillionaire yourself.

> *Try to surround yourself with people who share the same or better life goals and values as you do. People who inspire you. People who are already succeeding in the fields you want to succeed in. And see what will happen to you.*

Now, what would happen if your life partner and close group of friends are toxic people with no goals in life who complain all day about everything, talk nasty about others behind their backs, and lose their precious time on unworthy things? What would happen if they envy other people's wealth and success, lack self-confidence, and are in a bad mood most of the time? Imagine if *these* are the people with whom you spend the majority of your time and life. No matter how positive, goal-oriented, and wonderful you are, you will be affected and influenced by them, and unfortunately you will slowly change your behaviour to become exactly like them.

It's called *the power of influence.*

The more you are attached and close to someone—the more you interact with this person—the more this person has influence over you *without you even realizing it.*

It's *really* important to choose carefully whom you surround yourself with and with whom you spend the majority of your time and life.

Be aware that one of the most destructive things is to live with one or several toxic relationships. The closer the toxic person is to you, the worse you will be hurt. There are some toxic relationships that you can't cut out of your life because doing so may go against your morals or beliefs, but you must know that you will live with a burden deep inside yourself. A toxic relationship with a parent, a sibling, a life partner, or your own child is very hard to support and to live. But, you can protect yourself from negative impacts on you by knowing how to deal with the toxic person correctly.

If you do not have enough power to survive a relationship with a toxic person, then you can ask the help of a therapist who can give you great support in order to learn how to handle such people and relationships without harming yourself. Without help, it may be very difficult and can even destroy your life completely.

There are also great sources of information such as books, blogs, forums, videos that treat different aspects of living with a toxic person and overcoming a toxic relationship. Such resources can help you find ways to protect yourself and minimize the dangerous effects that those relationships can have on you.

> Toxic relationships can complete destroy your mental health and your entire life. Be aware who you let in your life.

However, I can tell you this: *The best way to minimize the impact of a toxic person on you is to distance yourself from that person once and for all, if possible. This is the real cure and the best remedy.*

Evaluate your relationships on a regular basis to know if they are good for you. Evaluate all the people around you and see if these are people you truly want to be in your life. Do they share the same life goals as you? If not, will they uplift you and encourage you to be who you want to be and to live the life you want to live? Will they influence you in a good way?

You want in your life positive and inspiring people who will elevate you as a person and with whom you will share great healthy relationships: people who will support you in your hard moments, be there for you in case something happens, celebrate you and celebrate life with you, and most important of all; love and respect you. You want to be around people who care about you and are *not* in your life to use and drain you or cause you to lose your precious time for their own benefit.

Keep in mind that healthy relationships always have ups and downs and people are not perfect. Anyone has good and bad things about them. No one is perfect. But be aware where you put yourself in. Once again awareness is key.

You can do this exercise several times a year to help you keep track of the quality of your entourage.

EXERCISE

1. Name the closest people to you—the ones with whom you interact the most.
2. On one side of each name, add a number (1 through 10) that shows how much positivity they bring you. (1—least positive; 10—most positive.)
3. Name the most toxic people in your life.
4. Can you cut contact with these people once and for all?
5. Name the people who you want to be around you forever.
6. Write a short description of qualities you want to find in new people you want to have in your life.

GOLDEN SECRET # 12

YOU CAN'T HAVE A SUCCESSFUL LIFE AND HEALTHY relationships if you don't *know* your boundaries, *set* them, *communicate* them, and *live* by them.

You could suffer in a relationship or in your life without knowing why. You could deal with major problems that exhaust you and in which you are completely absorbed—and you become so drained that you don't see the light anymore. Sometimes you put the blame on others around you or the situation for what happens. But the sad reality is that you are the one to blame.

You let that person or that situation put you through your troubles. It's because you did not set clear boundaries in the beginning of the relationship or that thing you decided to do in your life.

Why didn't you do that?

The answer is; because you lack self-love.

You let a person or situation cross your limits and now you feel only pain and suffering. And why, again? Because when you lack self-love, you lack self-respect. If you don't respect yourself enough, that will be reflected to others, and they will treat you the same way you treat yourself: with a lack of respect. The same goes for situations. If you did not know your limits and you did not set them at the beginning, you let that situation have control over you.

A lack of self-love is lack of self-worth, and that will result in a lack of self-knowledge and a lack of self-respect. When you love yourself, you know your worth, and you know what your boundaries are because you listen to yourself. You become aware of what your limits are with everyone and everything. And because you value and respect yourself, you want everyone around you to treat you with that same respect. This is the only way you will be able to communicate your boundaries and fight for them not to be crossed.

Sometimes you may know your boundaries, but because you lack self-love you don't dare communicate them, thinking instead that it will destroy your relationships or cause you to lose something or someone. With your own hands, you put your *self* in relationships and situations that treat you with disrespect and cross your limits. Because you are shy or too weak to affirm yourself and let everyone know your boundaries, you may cause your own emotional, physical, and maybe even financial downfall!

You may not know your boundaries. This also shows you lack self-love. Because as repeated many times already: the more you love yourself, the more you know yourself. In this situation, you must learn to know yourself in the first place—this is the only way you will know what your boundaries are and learn to set them appropriately.

Be conscious of your limits and boundaries and communicate them without being ashamed; this is the *only* way you will be treated the way you deserve to be treated. You have control of that; no one else does.

If you have high self-love already, and you know your boundaries, but you sometimes let them be crossed for whatever reason: don't forget to listen to yourself. There will always be ups and downs, so evaluate the situation you are in and take immediate action to avoid letting anyone cross your boundaries.

You are the only one who can communicate to the world so that it treats you the way you should be treated. This is your right. Don't give up on it.

Know your boundaries and communicate them without shame! You are valuable, you are worthy, and you deserve respect and love from yourself and everyone around you. *Never* forget that.

GOLDEN SECRET #13

ALL OUR LIVES WE SEARCH FOR THE PERFECT PARTNER WHO has already everything we dream about and with whom we think life will be finally wonderful just like in a fairy tale. We think that this person will come and magically improve our life. Until that time we feel void and unfulfilled and life has no taste at all. Yes it's good to look for a partner to share our life with but let me remind you of something. In the saying, *I have found my half,* it says you found your half, HALF, HALF.

It doesn't say your complete self.

You have found your half, which means someone who COMPLETES you and your already great and amazing life.

Yes, that is correct. Your life partner should complete you. He or she should be an addition to your actual happiness, something that you already have. He or she should complete everything in you.

You should form a team together and *share* life's beauty, not rely on one another for the basics in life. You should each be self-sufficient and complement one another.

A relationship between two partners is like a door lock. One person is the key and one person is the lock. To open the door, you need both. The key and lock are completely different, but when they are compatible, the mechanism is complete and functional—and the door opens!

Another crucial thing is to find someone *who loves you for who you truly are.*

Attracting someone in your life who loves you for who you are will first begin by acting and being your true self. Avoid presenting yourself as someone else to please a person you are attracted to or just to be liked because the fake version of yourself will eventually disappear because it is too difficult to keep up that charade for long periods of time.

If you act like someone else, then the person who falls in love with you will only love that *fake version*. Will he or she love the real you? No, because they won't even *know* the real you! So always stay authentic and true to yourself. And if someone doesn't accept the way you are then good for YOU ! You saved yourself from being in a bad relationship that can be ending with a broken heart.

Always be proud of who you are because there is someone out there in the world who is looking for the *real* you and to whom you are perfect just the way you are. This person will complete you and together you will experience the best that a relationship has to offer !

GOLDEN SECRET #14

SURELY YOU HAVE HEARD ABOUT THE *LAW OF ATTRACTION* because it was recently a huge trend. It was talked about everywhere.

The principle is that you attract what you think about the most. You learn to have a positive mindset, clear your negative thoughts, and visualize your desires in order to make them happen in real life.

Maybe you tried using the law of attraction and never got any results. Maybe you don't even believe it really exists!

Let me assure you: the law of attraction is working every single second of your life. It's a metaphysical law just like the law of gravity. It never stops working, and *it always* operates.

If it did not work for you even though you read all the books you could find and watched all the videos on YouTube about it, then here is what no one is telling you.

The real secret of the law of attraction is this: in order to make something happen you need to *not only* think about it, visualize it, say it to yourself as an affirmation, nor even have an everlasting positive mindset.

The real secret is that you need to believe your desire has *already happened* and feel the emotions as though your desire is *already yours* in real life. It's the constant and powerful belief in what you want becoming yours that will attract it, not only the thought nor the affirmation.

If you visualize it but don't *feel* the emotions that it brings you, then it's not going to work because you don't *believe* it. If you want it and think about it but you don't believe it, then it is never going to work.

You must constantly visualize yourself with your desire, daydream about it, think about the positive effect it will have on your life, and dream about it at night. You must truly believe it can and will happen.

The things you want to attract are not what comes to your mind only once in a while or just sometimes. You must crave them. When you crave something, you will think about it nonstop, and it will cause your unconscious actions to go toward that thing.

Visualize your desire. Visualization is not only seeing it in your mind's eye or dreaming about it. It's *living it* in your head and feeling the good emotions that it brings to you.

Believing is the biggest part of the deal. If your subconscious can't believe your goal, then you can't make it happen. You must have undeniable faith in it happening to be sure that your desire will come true.

Now you have the true method to make the law of attraction work, and you can start using it for everything to create the best version of yourself and your life.

EXERCISE

1. Name up to ten things you want to attract to your life in the short term.
2. Name up to ten things you want to attract to your life in the long term.

GOLDEN SECRET #15

YOUR ACTIONS DETERMINE WHO YOU ARE. IF YOUR ACTIONS are mainly good, you will be a good person with a good life who will attract good things to you!

Doing good is not only for others but also for yourself, too. No matter who it is for, no matter what it is, try to do good as much as possible.

However, doing good is not just your actions. It's also how you think, speak, and behave generally. No one is perfect and everyone makes mistakes, but try as much as you can to keep negative actions away from yourself. Behaving poorly sometimes is normal; we are human beings, not angels. But try to increase the good actions in everyday life, no matter how small that may be.

Another way to put it is to remind you of the Golden Rule, which you may have learned in grade school or even before: Do unto others as you would have them do unto you.

The reverse is also true. If you surround yourself with goodness and light, you will reciprocate that into the world.

When you start doing good with no expectation of anything in return, you will begin to see the goodness in other people as well; they are more likely to show it to you because you have been good first. Don't worry about grand gestures; think about good in small doses. It's the small things that make someone's day or ruin their mood. You may think you don't have enough money or time to put good into the world, but if you hold the door for someone else or help a woman with a stroller up the stairs, you will be making the world a better place, little by little.

This will elevate you as a person. Seeing yourself as a good person and making sure to do good will increase the love and respect you receive beyond your imagining.

Do good without asking anything in return. Do good freely for yourself and everyone.

What goes around, comes around! Creating good for yourself and others in your life will come back to you in positive ways that you never expected!

GOLDEN SECRET #16

One of the greatest success in life, you will learn, is helping to make other people successful. When you help someone, you change their life for the better. You show that person that there is hope in the world, and you are doing your part to perpetuate it. If you don't have anyone in your life who needs help, volunteer at a homeless shelter or donate to a humane society for example. Ask yourself where there is a need in your world and take action to help fill that need.

Everyone is different and when you see a person who needs help but you don't know what to do, ask them, and really *listen* to their answer. Listening to a person is a way of helping them in and of itself; it shows that you care about the other person and you are willing to focus on their struggle for a while.

Helping others will not only benefit others; it will benefit you the most.

When you are able to help someone without asking for something in return, you cultivate your own kindness. You will show yourself how good of a person you are; in today's world, nothing is free.

When you help someone else, you prove to your own self that you are a good human being and *you have value.* This increases your self-love and self-esteem. You'll increase self-respect, and it will help you feel proud of yourself.

Helping others who are in bad situations will also help you see that your problems and your struggles are small compared to what others must live through, and it will help you feel grateful for your problems and struggles instead of resenting them.

Imagine that you lost your job and you begin to think it's the end of the world and become depressed by that. Then, think about how your perspective would change if you went to help a single mom who just lost her child to cancer. That thing that seemed to have destroyed your life is comparatively benign when you think about how much worse it could be!

Go help someone. It can be at work, a shelter or food kitchen, school, or in your family. There is someone out there who needs the help you can give them. If you see yourself able to help that person, go out and do it. You can feel satisfied that you succeeded in accomplishing something great and changing someone's life.

When you help someone else solve their own problem, you are the first person to benefit from the situation because your unconscious mind will feel and understand that you have *succeeded* at something. You did something that the other person was not able to do on their own. It shows yourself that you are a skilled person and has a positive impact on how you see yourself. It will increase your self-confidence.

That is why you don't need to ask for something in return: you did something good for someone else *and* yourself. You feed yourself love, self-esteem, self-confidence, and self-worth without even realizing it.

GOLDEN SECRET #17

How many times have you been stuck in a promise that you made to someone on impulse? How many times have you found yourself drowning in a task that someone asked you to help them with when you have no time for yourself? How many times you found yourself losing important things such as time, money, or opportunities just to please someone? How many times you accepted a request and you didn't want to.

It's surely happened to you at least once in your life!

You may be a kind-hearted person and want to please everyone, or you may have a hard time refusing demands, or you may be around master manipulators and you can't say *no* to whatever request you receive.

We saw the importance of helping others and how much it can bring you on every level. But here are two important things you must remember.

1. You must help people who genuinely need your help.
2. You must help people without hurting or losing *yourself*.

Stop trying to please everyone around you. If you think they are using you and are capable of handling themselves, stop taking care of their responsibilities for them.

Let *no one* force you to lose your time, money, efforts, or opportunities. Do not accept a request unless it comes 100% from your heart. Never feel pressured by people asking you for unending requests; take courage and say ***NO***.

If you feel some people are abusing your generosity or you are completely lost in answering all the requests that come to you, then refuse politely.

The best solution to be able to say no and to stop pleasing everyone is; *self-love*! When you truly love yourself, you will prioritize yourself and refuse spend your energy on that which is unworthy. You will be able to say no without feeling guilty.

Try it once or twice, and you will see how much easier it is to choose to do only the things you truly accept and want to do and say *no* to the never-ending requests that may exhaust you!

GOLDEN SECRET #18

Your mental health is the root of your wealth, a beginning point for everything in your life.

If you are suffering mentally, it'll affect how you think, feel, and act. It will affect your physical health, your relationships, and everything else in your life.

We don't talk a lot about mental health. It's a little bit taboo. It's something we can't see with our eyes, so sometimes it's hard for us to understand it or even acknowledge its existence. Even if we can't see it, it's still the biggest part of us.

It's like your soul: you can't see it, but it's *you*.

Because of our lack of understanding, we may feel pain in our bodies and tend to put it aside like we are just physically ill. We see any physical imbalance as a *body* response to our daily stress or unhealthy habits, but we rarely associate it with a mental disorder or illness. We tend to assume that someone who is mentally ill is simply a crazy person. In fact, that's false.

> Your mental health is so powerful that *a mental disorder can actually lead to a physical illness.*

Did you know that your body reflects your mental health state ?

Your mental health is *at least* as important as your physical health—if not even more so. Simply put, what's in your mind will manifest in your body. If you are mentally healthy and balanced, then your body will follow. If you are mentally ill, the consequences will be shown in your body. You will age faster and be more prone to severe physical troubles such as diabetes, high cholesterol, cardiac problems, and even cancer.

Your life experience, the way you think, and your emotional reactions are like food for your mental health. And what happens when you feed yourself nasty food? You got it!

The way you think and feel about yourself, others, life, and everything will affect your mental health in either a good or bad way. Starting in your childhood, the traumas, emotions, and beliefs you have acquired and held within you all this time will show themselves in your mental health today—*and in and on your body.*

Life is not perfect for anybody, and we all have mental health issues. No one is completely, 100% healthy, mentally *or* physically. It's important to be aware of your mental health because it has a huge impact over your physical condition and your life. Having good mental health is the basis for a good physical health, healthy relationships, and a life that flourishes.

Just like when you see your primary physician for a regular check-up, it is crucial that you take the time to determine whether you suffer from any mental illness, small or large. This will not only help you see clearer, it may illuminate for you why certain things happen to you on a physical level or why you struggle in relationships, at work, or at school.

I encourage you to read good books about mental health and start cultivating knowledge about it. Talk about it with friends and family and spread the word. Maybe there are people around you who are struggling. If you are in poor mental health, I strongly suggest that you consult a specialist to talk about it. He or she will help you identify the exact things that are causing problems that affect your mental health and can give you ways to work on those things in order to heal.

You must take the time to do it, like a blood test, to know if your overall health is okay because it's the starting point of everything else in your life. Being in good mental health is the basis of being the best version of yourself—everything else will follow.

GOLDEN SECRET #19

Your time is the most precious thing you own. It can never be replaced or given again, and when you lose it, you can never get it back.

A lost day, a lost week, a lost month, or a lost year in your life is something that you will never *ever* get back.

Learn to spend and invest time in things that will make the most of the time you have been given.

You may think you have plenty of time in front of you, so there is no urgent need to start doing what you need or want to do. You put everything aside because you don't see the value of the time you have in that moment. You don't acknowledge the real value of it. If you lose that precious time and don't think frequently on how you are spending it, then you may wake up one day with no recompense. Instead, you will feel guilty for the rest of your life for not grabbing the opportunity you had when you had it.

The best way to avoid losing time and to make the most of what you have is to actually evaluate what you are doing *every single day of your life.*

When you wake up in the morning (or even the night before!), ask yourself what your day is going to look like. Make a plan of how you want your day to go. When your day is over just before going to sleep, evaluate how you did. Did you do as much from your plan as you could? Or did you lose your day to things not worthy of your time?

Your plans can be about reaching your goals or even just enjoying free time. If you want to climb Mount Everest, then do so. If you want to stay in bed all day instead, then do that. The most important thing is that you spend your time wisely and enjoy the time spent.

Time is like a currency: spend it well.

Evaluate your time spent on a regular basis and on the long term. Briefly recap each day, week, month, and year. Time flies so fast that sometimes a whole year may pass, and you are still stuck on a small thing you haven't yet begun.

Don't allow anyone else to use your time or spend it as they wish without your consent. Your time is *your* time, and *you* have full control over it. Don't give it freely; guard it jealously. Your time should *always* bring you something in return, if not money then pleasure or anything else you see as worthy of having in this life. You own your own time, so make it your best asset, use it to your advantage, and taste its fruits!

GOLDEN SECRET #20

WE ALL LOOK FOR PERFECTION IN ALL AREAS OF OUR LIVES. We expect perfection in everything. Even if each one of us has our own standard of perfection, we still seek it in our lives. This is something completely natural and normal.

We want our appearance, love life, health, family, career, relationships, and everything to be perfect. Maybe you're saying to yourself right now, "Oh, no. I never look for perfection; I *know* nothing is perfect."

Nevertheless, unconsciously, you want perfection in yourself and your life. Like the rest of us, you are surrounded with stimulation and advertising that make you unconsciously want the unattainable.

Acknowledge—truly acknowledge—the fact that nothing and no one is perfect.

Not only does perfection not exist, but what we see as perfect will never stay perfect, if it ever was in the first place. This holds true for your own self as well. Don't put pressure on yourself to be perfect for anyone, even yourself. You are who you are. What makes you perfect is your imperfections!

Don't build your self-confidence on a perfect image or standards that are so high that you cannot possibly reach them. That is like building a house on quicksand. You don't have to be perfect for society or even for someone in particular. No one makes the rules for you except *you*.

Maybe you are at a point in your life where you don't value yourself because you don't have the perfect body, career, or life partner, and this deeply affects your self-confidence and self-worth. Maybe you put yourself under a lot of pressure in order to accomplish things that you think will create perfection around you! Rest assured: nothing is or will ever be perfect.

Stop stressing about perfection. Let it be. Learn to see the beauty in imperfection. Free yourself from the negative desire that is holding you back from seeing the beauty in yourself and your life just the way they are.

GOLDEN SECRET #21

WITH EVERY BREATH YOU TAKE, YOU MAKE A CHOICE. Everything is a choice, starting with what you think today to what you eat three days from now to where you will live ten years from now.

You are the only one in control of yourself, so you are the only one who has control over your choices.

Maybe you are in a situation in which you did not choose to be, and you feel that you are stuck, so you say to yourself, "This will never change. I have no choice but to accept it and stay like this."

I have no choice... These four words make you a prisoner in a prison of your own design.

Whether or not you believe it, you always have a choice. ALWAYS.

But it's true that sometimes you don't have an *easy* choice. All the choices in front of you may be so difficult that they make you think you have *no* choice at all. If it feels like you have no power over changing a situation or like making a choice will give you even bigger problems, it's okay. Don't force yourself to make a hard choice if you are not ready to commit to it and may not be able to handle the result. Don't stress.

Let's say you are in a very toxic relationship that was built years ago, and you are stuck in it today. Each time you decide to leave, it becomes a huge issue that leads to very big problems, so instead you become a prisoner of that person and that relationship. You *can* leave, but the process would be so detrimental that you could not handle it. Instead, you stay in the relationship because you think you have no other choice. It's okay; this is *your* choice.

Even if you *are* stuck in a toxic relationship that is killing you and you can't physically leave, you still have the choice to control your feelings. You could stop being emotionally dependant upon that person and the trauma they cause you. You could detach yourself completely until that person has no mental or emotional effect on you. You could create happiness by surrounding yourself with things you love and do activities that provide you happiness and that help to detach you from the trauma in which you are living. Be patient and detach yourself mentally and emotionally until you are ready to physically detach yourself from that person, with or without the drama you feared would happen.

Another example is your health. Your health is the reflection of your choices (unless, of course, you have a disease you were born with). Your health, your weight, and the overall state of your body is a result of the choices you make every single day. You choose every day what you eat, and whether you're going to participate in some form of physical fitness or not. If you are overweight and your health is in a bad condition, you can choose to change your unhealthy habits. It's your *choice*.

Your career is also a result of your choices. Even if you are not happy with the career you have today, it was still a result of your choices. But remember: you can *choose* today to make a change.

You have the ability and right to make your own choices.

Don't let anyone or anything influence your choices. Let them come from *you*. When you make choices, anticipate the good and the bad that will come from them and *think* before acting. If something is bothering you or you are not satisfied with something in your life, *then choose to make change.*

It's never too late to make new choices that will lead you to a better place. You are alive, and you have this opportunity every single day! So, grab it today!

EXCERISE

1. Write three choices you regularly make that make your life difficult.
2. Write three choices you can change that will immediately improve your life.
3. Write five choices you made in the past that led you to a bad situation.
4. Write five choices you can make *now* that will improve your future.

GOLDEN SECRET #22

PRIORITIZING YOURSELF IS NOT ABOUT BEING SELFISH AND neglecting everyone else. Not at all. It's about putting yourself first, loving yourself, and caring for yourself in order for you to be able to be there for others.

Your *self* is your mind, body, and soul.

You may say that you are fully occupied by your work, educational studies, responsibilities, family tasks, partner, or kids and you don't have *time* to prioritize yourself. You may actually be convinced that it's a *crime* to put yourself first.

But here is a question: if you lose yourself, your body is burned out, your mind is suffering, and you become ill, are you going to be able to keep up with your work, responsibilities, family, kids or projects?

The answer is a definitive *no*. When you lose yourself and you are not fulfilled, you can't fulfil anyone else!

If you lose yourself, you lose it all. In order to give the best of yourself in everything you do in life, you have to be in good a good state physically and mentally. To do *that*, you must prioritize yourself.

Before giving yourself entirely to someone or something, think about it. And then think about it again.

If you sacrifice yourself for someone, will that person have the power to give you back what you lost for them? That is, your energy, time, health, youth, beauty, or inner peace? Unfortunately, *no*, not even if they tried. They can be grateful to you and support you in whatever ways they can, but they may not! Why take a chance on that? (The same thing applies in a given situation if you don't prioritize yourself.)

In order to avoid that happening, always think about yourself. Remember to put yourself first and avoid neglecting the things you do for yourself, the self-care for your body and mind.

Always fulfil yourself first so that you *can* fulfil others and your obligations. Take care of yourself so that you *can* succeed in everything you do. Avoid losing yourself entirely so that you don't wake up one day with irreparable damage to your person.

GOLDEN SECRET #23

Your home is the house of your body. Likewise, your body is the house of your mind and soul.

If your house (the place where you live) is dirty, a mess, not well put together, and not in good repair, then how would you feel? *Bad.*

It's the same thing for your mind and soul. How do you expect to feel in an unhealthy, dirty, and not-well-cared-for body? *Bad*, of course.

After your mental health, your physical health and wellbeing is your number one priority. Your physical health is a reflection of your mental health as seen earlier. If you are sick mentally and suffer from mental or emotional trauma, then this will show in your countenance and physique, and it will have negative effects on your overall physical health. It may even affect your physical beauty and you can age quicker.

But the reverse is also true. The state of your body has a big impact on the state of your mind. You may be in great mental health and be emotionally well, but if you neglect taking care of your body by always eating unhealthy food, not getting good sleep and having a stressful lifestyle, you will exhaust yourself and start to see bad things happen within your mind as well.

The first step to taking care of your body is to take care of your mental health and balance your emotions.

Then, you must feed your body with healthy nutrients, sleep well, adequately hydrate, and exercise regularly. This should be a *lifestyle*, not just a temporary diet for a special event or summer. Live a healthy lifestyle so that you will have enough energy and resistance to do whatever you want in life. Plus, you will always look and feel beautiful.

When you look and feel your best, you perform your best. And when you perform your best, you attract the best!

Take good care of your body and make this a habit. Invest time and money in your physique because it is the best investment you will ever make. Your body is your property. You own your body your entire life: you want it to be in the best shape ever!

Love your body by appreciating it. No matter it's shape, size, or actual state, love your body and be proud of it. There is nothing more important in the world than your health and the state of your body plays an important part in that, so don't neglect it.

GOLDEN SECRET #24

YOUR MIND IS THE TRUE REFLECTION OF EVERYTHING YOU are on a physical level. And, like your body, you can take care of it by feeding it, cleaning it, working on it, and loving it.

The more you foster learning in yourself, the more you will mentally grow. You don't need to have a PhD or high grades in school or a lot of life experience to have a cultivated mind. You only need to be open to lifelong learning.

Lifelong learning is food for your mind.

You are never too old to learn something new and nurture yourself. Life is a journey, and each step has an experience from which you can learn. You went to school where you learned a lot. You work, so you have earned new skills and experience. But it doesn't stop there.

Just because you are a doctor doesn't mean you can't also be an artist. And vice versa. Your mind has unlimited power to learn and absorb things to an unimaginable degree! You can learn as many skills as you want, and your mind will never ever experience long-term fatigue. It is your body that is limited, not your mind.

The mind is an endless source of power that can be used without limit!

Acquire new knowledge in new fields in order to feed yourself in all areas of your life and through your life experience. It can be as simple as learning a new recipe, how to draw, how to sew, how to sing, how to... *anything*! You can learn about psychology, medicine, metaphysics, and more. There is no limit to what you can learn, and with today's technology, information is available like never before. Read books, try new activities, or take an online course in a field you like.

Feeding your mind will develop your knowledge base, improve your lexicon, and open the door of unlimited possibilities. You never know what you'll get out of what you learn; maybe you'll be able to quit your job and start your own business in something new you learned that has no connection with your previous field. You just don't know!

Make a small, continuous effort in your education—conventional or otherwise—and see how powerful you become. Knowledge will enrich your life, relationships, and conversations. No doubt you will be amazed by your own limitless mind!

GOLDEN SECRET #25

CONNECT WITH YOURSELF ON A DEEPER LEVEL THAN connecting with your mind, thoughts, and emotions. Nurture your spirituality and connect with your *soul*. Learn about it and speak with it. Detach yourself from the materialistic world and go on a journey to discover your true self and the true meaning and purpose of your life.

The more time you take to connect with your soul and encourage your spirituality, the easier life will become for you because you will connect with a powerful force that will guide you through everything in life in a magical and divine way.

The more you connect with yourself on a spiritual level, the easier life will seem to you. The less your problems affect you, the more peaceful you'll become. The spiritual force you seek will give you light, hope, patience, force, and power over everything.

Spirituality is the true power. It will always guide you to the destination you need most.

Take a moment to connect with your soul on a deep level. Cultivate your spirituality and enjoy the amazing benefits of it.

The soul itself is a spiritual thing. It is commonly held to be distinct from your body; it is the spiritual, moral part of humans, believed to survive death. Often, it is regarded as being the emotional part of a person—the seat of feelings or sentiments. While the mind is logical and intellectual, the soul is emotional and spiritual. When someone says, "I can see into your soul," what they mean is they know you on the deepest, most intimate level, whether that be for good or ill.

There's something to be said for taking a walk out in a field of wild flowers or letting your bare feet sink deep into the sand at the beach or listening to the rain on your rooftop as you drift off to sleep. These are powerful, spiritual things, and the world is full of them. Have you ever watched a spider create its web? Have you ever planted a vegetable from seed and watched it grow as you cared for it day after day? When you connect with your soul, you begin to focus on being present in your own body in the world as it is every day instead of rushing from one thing to the next, trying to catch up or slow down without ever so much as catching your breath!

Close your eyes and take a deep breath. Take a little time out of the day for yourself, and notice how you feel. How do you feel emotionally? Are you feeling worn out or taxed or elated? How do you feel in your body? Do you feel heavy or light? Are you tense anywhere? Where? Can you think of a reason why that might be?

Remember this: *the solutions to life's biggest problems and the answers to all your questions are hidden in your soul.*

GOLDEN SECRET #26

YOU WORK HARD FOR THE BEST CAREER, THE BEST GRADES IN school, the highest socioeconomic status, and all the best life achievements.

But your *greatest* accomplishment is none of those things. Your greatest accomplishment is, in fact, *inner peace*.

You may receive everything you ever dreamed of and worked so hard for, but you will feel always unfulfilled without inner peace.

Inner peace is a powerful source of happiness.

Everything you accomplish in life should lead you to inner peace. It's the best way to savour what you acquire and be genuinely happy. When you want something or someone in your life, consider whether this thing or person will bring you inner peace. If not, then it's not worth having in your life.

What is inner peace? Also known as *peace of mind*, inner peace is the intentional state of psychological or spiritual calm, even in the face of stress. It's a healthy alternative to anxiety, depression, and irrational anger. Associated with bliss, contentment, and happiness, inner peace is considered by many to be the state in which a person's mind is optimized for positive performance.

A person may have difficulty embracing their inner self because trauma, societal change, or everyday stressors get the best of them; don't let this be you! I am not saying it's easy, but take every day on its own terms—do the best you can with what you have been given and keep your mental health in mind—and you will begin to see things fall into place for you. When you practice meditation, breathing exercises, or prayer each day consistently, you will find the true source of happiness has actually been inside you all along. It doesn't need to take a lot of time—maybe half an hour to an hour every day at most—but you will discover the benefits in every part of your life: health, career, family, friends, and more.

It is okay to want physical comforts and material wealth in life; just make sure that's not all you want! When you connect your goals and aspirations to your peace of mind, you will better be able to see what is good for you and moving you in the right direction and what is not.

Let inner peace be your real goal in life; always keep it in mind and let it dictate your actions.

GOLDEN SECRET #27

Here the best advice you will ever receive on self-confidence:

Never build your self-confidence on people's good opinions of you, your intelligence, your skills, your talent, your beauty, your money, your youth, your fame, the car you drive, the house where you live, or your successes because the day you lose one of them is the day you lose your self-confidence, too!

Self-confidence comes from within. Even if you don't possess anything but your own self, you can be self-confident because self-confidence comes from self-love.

Now, you may be asking yourself, "What is self-confidence, and how can I become self-confident?"

There are two kinds of thoughts and beliefs you have in your mind about yourself. You have one or the other in your mind right know, whether or not you know it. (Sorry; there is no in between.) You are most of the time not aware of those thoughts because they are processed in your subconscious mind. But they are behind all your conscious decisions and actions in life.

If you have low self-confidence, you think and believe like this:

I hope everyone likes me. I do things to attract attention.

I hope everyone is proud of me. I hope everyone will cheer my successes and admire me. I will do things in my life so people see how great I am. I need to be perfect and I need to follow what everyone does so I can fit in and be approved. I have to talk, walk, dress, eat, and think like everyone else. I must follow the trends. I am scared everyone will see my imperfections and they will not like me because of them.

I care about what others think of me. I love myself depending on how much others love me.

But if you have high self-confidence, you think and believe like this:

I don't care if anyone else likes me because *I* like me! I don't need to attract attention because I am already fabulous and shine like a star in the sky!

I don't care if everyone is proud of me because *I* am proud of me. I don't care if no one cheer my successes and admires me—I do everything for myself. I already know how great I am and don't need anyone to tell me that. I don't need to be perfect; I accept myself as I am. I don't need to follow what everyone else does so that I can fit in or be approved. I talk, walk, dress, eat, and think as I want. I don't follow trends; I follow my own taste. I love my imperfections because they make me special and unique!

It doesn't matter what others think of me. I love myself just the way I am!

That's it. To be truly self-confident, you must love yourself and completely *internalise* the second inner monologue.

GOLDEN SECRET #28

L̲ife is about finding balance.̲ M̲aybe you heard that before: maybe it's already a life goal to be balanced or maybe this is the first time you've ever heard of it.

You may be living with extremes in some or all areas of your life. And truly: that is exhausting. Maybe you are not balanced because you are a kind of person who sees only "black and white" and you go from one extreme to another in all your choices and actions. Maybe it's all or nothing for you. That is not a problem; you just have to work on finding a balance within yourself and in the outside world.

The more balanced you are mentally, physically, and emotionally, the more you will be able to enjoy a balanced life and avoid extremes. The extreme you want to avoid is the negative one especially! Being balanced will keep you away from that.

Everything in your life should be balanced, from your relationships to your work to the way you eat and sleep. *Everything*.

Balance is something that you need to work for; it's not something that necessarily comes naturally and it takes a lot of self-discipline. Make it a goal for yourself.

EXERCISE

1. Name ten things in your life that are at an extreme and lacking balance.
2. What can you do today to help balance out these extremes?

GOLDEN SECRET #29

HAVE YOU EVER EXPERIENCED A MOMENT IN YOUR LIFE WHEN you didn't care about something happening and it easily came to you just way you wanted? Or the opposite: when you stressed about something happening and it just turned out very bad?

Of course, *yes*! I don't know anyone who hasn't.

If you have no control over something, do what you can to influence it, and let the universe take care of the rest. If it's meant to happen, it will happen. Of course, I am not saying don't go after your dreams and goals, but don't let them be touched by negativity and complaints. As the saying goes, you catch more flies with honey than vinegar, and this is true in life, too! When you stress over something so much that you become physically ill or paranoid, you are doing yourself and those around you a disservice. You are putting harmful thoughts and actions into the world, and you will see and experience only damage and conflict in return. Relax! Take a deep breath. Imagine good things coming to you instead.

Think of it this way. Pretend you are walking on a sandy beach, and you bend down to scoop up a handful of sand. Do you hold the sand as tightly in your fist as possible? No, of course not! If you do that, the sand will literally slip through your fingers. But if you hold the sand in the cup of your hand without trying too hard to hold it, you will be able to hold much more of it than you would in your closed fist. Your life is like the sand on the beach. It is okay and even admirable to scoop up some for yourself, but don't hold it too tightly or you will lose most of it through your clenched fingers.

When you want something to happen so badly that you stress about it and focus only on what could go wrong, you are unconsciously sending negativity toward that thing. Sending out negativity is bad for yourself *and* the situation. You're making the chance much lower that it'll happen positively, and you are actually encouraging the situation to happen with problems!

For example: externally, you want your relationship with your romantic partner to be beautiful forever, but internally you stress about keeping it perfect and become afraid of losing it altogether. So, you start asking "What if...?" in your head, have suspicions about things that don't exist, and create problems without good reason. You begin to argue and fight with your partner about things you created in your own mind. And eventually, you end up destroying your relationship with your own hands!

Why must you inflict on yourself so much negative stress in order to make things happen exactly the way you want? Why must you over-analyse everything and everyone day and night? Why don't you just *let it go* and *let it be*?

There *are* things over which you have no control, so let them go. Let them be as they are. Don't force anything.

Free yourself from the anxiety of trying to make things perfect or happen in exactly the way you want. Accept your flaws; accept defeat gracefully; accept loss and anticipate how to deal with it before it happens. Don't burn out trying to fit things into your perfect vision.

Do this *as a gift to yourself*. Stop forcing the issue and stressing about everything that's not perfectly the way you want. Do what you have to do, of course, but let things happen naturally without putting extra pressure on those things or people.

Go with the flow. Don't force things, and you will see how light you become without the anxiety bringing you down!

GOLDEN SECRET #30

WE ALL WANT TO LOVE AND BE LOVED, AND WE ALL ADMIRE others and seek the admiration of others. Our whole lives, we try to impress and seek attention and admiration from everyone around us. This behaviour began when we were babies with our own parents. Now adults, we still want others and the world to approve of us so we can fit in, create relationships, and bond.

Seeking attention shows that we exist as human beings. When others notice us, approve of us, admire us, and love us, we feel alive.

Admiration is a form of love, which is why human beings need it. With admiration comes love and affection. We feed our souls with love, and we can't live without love. It is not a bad thing to want people to admire us and give us attention—it's human nature. When we accomplish our goals and dreams and succeed in something and people show us love and applaud us because of that, we feel encouraged to continue pursuing our goals and dreams. It's a natural form of motivation that helps us feel important.

It only becomes bad when we live only for that. When we live *only* to prove ourselves to others and *only* accomplish things to seek attention and admiration, *then* it becomes a problem. When we need and crave attention to the point where we feel depressed and dead inside when we are not noticed, something is very wrong. If attention and favour from others becomes our only motivation, it begins to be obvious our lives are not balanced as they should be.

You may recognize yourself in this, or you may be partaking only occasionally.

In either case, it's a toxic behaviour because you build your self-worth, self-love, self-confidence, and self-esteem on what others think of you instead of learning and growing those things from the inside out. And if you make it a habit and learn to love yourself based on what people think about you and how people see you, you set yourself up for failure.

The moment you don't get attention for your accomplishments or you receive negative comments, you will be completely broken down.

Additionally, you may push or force yourself to do things you don't want to do just to get attention or impress someone. This will certainly exhaust you mentally, physically, and emotionally. If you let it, it can become an obsessive behaviour and you won't be able to stop.

You should not need to prove yourself to any other human being on Earth. *Prove yourself only to yourself.*

When you accomplish something, practice making *yourself* happy first. Don't wait for someone to praise you to feel accomplished and confident and powerful. Self-confidence is key because the more you are confident in yourself, the less you will seek others' approval and admiration. Everything you do should be for *you*.

Here's a question: are you in a situation where you are killing yourself to impress someone else? It may be a lover, a friend, a parent, someone at work, or even a whole society! Okay, so what would happen if you *did* prove yourself to that person? Are you any better off than you were before?

Think about it and meditate on it.

Be a powerful, self-confident person, and only do things you love for yourself—not to prove yourself to anyone else!

EXERCISE

1. Name five things you are doing right now to get approval or impress someone.
2. Are those things you genuinely love doing, or are you forcing yourself to do them?
3. If you stop doing those things, will you lose the love and admiration of the people from whom you are seeking this form of love?
4. Do these things positively feed you on a personal level?
5. If not, can you stop doing them immediately?

(If you could not think of any answer for question A, then I congratulate you!)

GOLDEN SECRET #31

WE ALL WANT ACCEPTANCE AND APPROVAL. SOMETIMES WE don't embrace our real selves, fearing that others will judge us because we do not meet the societal standards that a majority of people follow. We feel like we have to be the *same* as everyone around us in order to fit in—we worry that we must dress, think, and talk the same and have similar goals, tastes, values, and points of view in order to be accepted.

If *you* feel that you need to be like everyone else in your entourage or in society to be accepted and feel appreciated, then it's time for you to start changing that belief right now! If you're *acting* based on this belief by presenting yourself as someone else, imitating others, and not being authentic just to gain acceptance and approval from everyone else, *please stop immediately.*

When you are authentic and true to your inner self, you will attract people who love you for those reasons instead of liking the "you" you present to them. In fact, people in general tend to like an authentic person more than a person perceived as fake or phony. So, what is it about authenticity that's so critical? Well, it's important to hold your beliefs and values in high esteem. Of course, it's okay to change your mind after careful consideration, but sticking to your guns even in the face of adversity or peer pressure is one indicator of authenticity. (Think of the classic movie *12 Angry Men* as a great example of this.)

Another indicator of authenticity is passion. What are you passionate about? It may be that you love teaching or you want to save the Earth or protect endangered animals. Dig deep and think about what you actually care about—what you *truly* care about—and you'll find your passion. Maybe you love knitting hats for dogs or playing golf or collecting heart-shaped rocks. What would you do if you didn't need to work? What do you do because you're obsessed with it? *That's* your passion.

But conviction and passion aren't the only things you need to be an authentic person. According to scientists, you must also have realistic perceptions of reality (no delusions of grandeur, for instance), be accepting of yourself and other people, be thoughtful, have a non-hostile sense of humour, be able to express your emotions freely and clearly, and be open to learning from your own mistakes.

If you don't want to travel to Bali, then don't go! Just because everyone is going and tagging themselves in pictures on social media doesn't mean you have to go, too! If you want to go to Madagascar instead, then go there! It may not be fancy or exotic like Bali, but it has its own draw, and you should go there if you're drawn to it, no matter what anyone else says.

Yes, of course you want to be accepted; this is non-negotiable and completely normal. Wanting acceptance from others is not the problem here. The problem is that you may be trying to be someone you're not while in pursuit of that acceptance. You want *real*, genuine acceptance and true love and admiration from others. *For that, you must be genuine and authentic.*

Own your differences; own your uniqueness. It is what makes you special and unique, like no one else in this world. If someone won't accept you for who you truly are, then they don't belong in your life. You only need the people who love you for you; *they* will give you authentic love. And they will accept the real you.

Don't worry about trying to fit in—you are amazing just the way you are. Be authentic and shine!

GOLDEN SECRET #32

When we are on social media, we think life is perfect for everyone except us!

When we surf social media, we see people apparently living perfect lives all day every day. Everything we see seems to be perfect. And here *we* are, sitting in our pyjamas watching other people swimming among the sea shells, eating macarons in Paris, driving the best cars, wearing the best clothes, getting in shape and having fit bodies, living their best lives ever.

Your first reaction may be to compare yourself with what you see. But remember this: no one puts the negative side of their life on the internet. What you see is a person's successes, not their failures; their travel, not their day job; their best moments, not their worst.

It's difficult not to compare your whole self with what you see because where everyone is and what everyone has is way too far from where you are and what you have. What you see is dreams and life goals for you. And you may think to yourself that you will never achieve what others have. You may feel like you lack things in your life. You may think that what you see is *normal* and *standard* and *basic* and that you are so far away from that.

It may even create self-image and self-worth issues without your even realizing it. This is true even if you don't follow popular people—let's say you only have access to your own circle of friends. What will appear on your social media feed is only your friends' successes, travels, and best moments. *No one puts their whole self on the internet—they only put their best self.*

You see your friends living their best lives, accomplishing things, buying houses and cars, having wonderful relationships, and so on. *But you are only seeing the good side of it.*

> We are tangentially aware that social media is a perfected reality that doesn't really exist.

If *you* are affected by this, here is a good remedy: Begin to see social media as *motivation* and *inspiration*—not as a threat. Make all the people you admire on social media role models and start improving yourself and your life. Slowly, you will begin to see your reality become better, and you won't feel like you are less than any other human being.

You must also acknowledge that the perfection you see on social media is only a *part* of people's lives. No matter how perfect they may look to you, everyone struggles with *some*thing in their lives.

Beautify your real life as you wish, and use social media as motivation and inspiration to create the best version of yourself and your life!

GOLDEN SECRET #33

I WANT YOU TO ASK YOURSELF THIS QUESTION: "Do I *genuinely* love what I am doing in my life?"

This is a question you should ask yourself daily, each morning and night.

Surely there is *some*thing in your life that you do without truly loving it.

Why do we keep doing things we don't love? Why must we study a field we hate, work in a job we double hate, and live a life we triple hate? Why must we always choose according to what will bring us acceptance? Worse than that, why must we inflict on ourselves things we don't like?

Why do we do things just so that we are accepted? We wear clothes we don't like, eat things we don't like, do activities we don't like, follow education we don't like, stay with partners we don't like, and work jobs we don't like!

Or maybe we do things we don't like doing because we feel it is the right thing to do, because it is part of our beliefs. We were raised with certain beliefs and values that our parents entrusted to us and we may feel that we have to follow those beliefs, but in fact we find ourselves doing things we hate and living a life we hate!

For example: if you were raised in a family of doctors and you have a belief that you must become a doctor to succeed in life, but you would actually prefer to become a hair stylist, then go toward becoming a hair stylist instead! Don't impose something you don't love on yourself. You never know, your family may not even know your preference! You may not even receive any familial pressure; the pressure to fit in can sometimes come from yourself.

Do what you genuinely love in *everything* because it's the only way you will truly succeed and love your life.

Doing something you don't love will only make you hate yourself and your life. If you receive an education in a field you don't like because you are seeking you parent's approval, you are wasting your time. If you hate that field of work, then chances are you won't succeed in it after you graduate, and you will lose precious time and effort—if not your life!

Don't work in a job you don't like just because it brings you more money. Each day will be a punishment, and you will not perform your best. When you quit, you will have lost so much time and energy. If you don't quit, you will burn yourself out.

When you study in or work doing something you love, you don't see it as a work anymore. Instead, it becomes a part of you. You don't feel pressure to produce because you are already producing naturally the fruit of your love.

Do only what you genuinely love, what motivates you and makes you happy, even if it's not in everyone's taste. You may even seem crazy to some people, and they may not accept you. Be who you are, even if it doesn't quite fit in with the beliefs you were taught in childhood. Own it, and do only what gives you pleasure and inner peace.

In relationships, don't force yourself to do things you don't like just keep that relationship. Discuss your concerns with the other person and find a middle ground. If there is no middle ground, then maybe that's not a good relationship for you. I ask you a question: how can you love your relationship if you are forced most of the time to do things you don't like? Stand up for yourself, and avoid doing things just to please another person. Make sure you get satisfaction for yourself, too!

Begin all actions and make all choices based on love. When you genuinely love every aspect of your life, you will love your life as well!

EXERCISE

1. Name five things you do daily that you don't like doing.
2. Name five things you love but do *not* do daily.
3. Name three reasons why you can't do the things you love.
4. Do you love your job? Are you in love with your career choices?
5. Do you love the choices you make on a daily basis?
6. What actions can you take today in order to start doing what you really love in life?

GOLDEN SECRET #34

WE ALL DO IT! AND YOU SURELY DO IT ALSO: *NEVER ENDING comparison. And it's like drinking poison for your soul.*

That is slowly killing your self-confidence without your even realizing it. You may even be doing it unconsciously.

Do you compare every single thing in your body with people you find more attractive? Or do you compare your romantic relationship with your friends' around who seem like they are living "happily ever after"s? Do you compare your income with people who make more money than you or compare your skills with everyone else's? You keep comparing, comparing, and comparing. And of course you come up lacking.

With those comparisons, you diminish yourself. You see yourself lower than what you see in other people. This directly affects your self-confidence. Plus, it also focuses you on only the things you *lack* in yourself and your life and not on the good qualities and things you have.

Never let the things you want make you forget the good things you have.

When you compare yourself to others and find yourself lacking, you are actually being ungrateful for what you already have. Remember, the more grateful you are, the more you will receive things to be grateful for. But the reverse is also true: the less grateful you are, the more likely you will be to lose the good things you have in your life.

Comparing yourself to others is a habit that you must stop *immediately*. If you don't, you will continue to feel intimidated and diminished by everyone around you. No one's life is perfect, and you know it! Please keep this in your mind always.

Avoid comparing yourself with everyone else, be grateful for the good things you have, and work to improve yourself and your own life.

If you still want to compare yourself to someone, here is the only type of person you may compare yourself to: someone who has *peace of mind*. Focus on that person, and seek that same thing she has. If you can ask her how he or she does it, then do so. Be *inspired* by that person. Among all other things in this life, you should be striving for peace of mind; everything else that people possess cause only temporary satisfaction.

Why compare yourself with someone who has something "better" than you when the universe is full of possibilities and you already know that you can make everything you want yours?

GOLDEN SECRET #35

Fear is your biggest enemy!

You must distance yourself from it as much as possible. Fear is one thing that is stopping you from receiving everything good into your life.

Fear is something that holds you back and sticks you in your situation without any possibility for growth or change.

You may say, "Easier said than done!" That may be, but if you free your mind from fear, then nothing will be difficult for you anymore. Take a moment to control your fear—I want you to start by thinking that it's possible.

You have power over your emotions because you are the only one who is feeding them with your thoughts!

Here is how to overcome your fear, whatever it may be of:

Imagine your fear as *real*. (Even though it's not a good feeling, you must do this.) Imagine for a moment that your greatest fear actually happens in real life.

Now, imagine how you would react to it and how it would affect you. Try to imagine your true reaction, even if you feel overwhelmed by it. Have you died from what you feared the most, or are you still alive?

Unless your greatest fear is death itself, you are alive! You *survive* your greatest fear.

Your fear is the fruit of your imagination, and you have total control over it. You can amplify it or make it disappear. If you decide to amplify it and to live with it every day, then what is most likely to happen? *You will bring it into your life.* Remember: that which you think about the most is that which you attract to your life. This is the law of attraction. Let's discuss it again briefly!

If you live every single day with the fear of losing your job, so much that it hinders your ability to work, then guess what will happen? *You will lose your job.* If you fear that your partner will cheat on you so much that you withdraw from the relationship or wrongfully accuse him of such, then guess what? *Your partner will cheat on you.* When your conscious mind thinks about something, your subconscious mind saves that information and you will act in that direction without even realising it.

Your fears operate in two ways: first, they stop you from evolving—when you take action, they hold you back. With fear in your heart and mind, you will lack confidence and possibly fail in what you are doing. Second, if you focus on your fear, you will attract it into your life.

The real secret to fighting your fears is to find a possible solution for them or find a positive outcome—a silvering lining, so to speak—if they were to happen. If there is a solution and a silver lining, then *bingo*! Your fears won't have the same impact on you anymore because now you know how to handle them. You have *power* over your fear.

You created your fears, so you are the only one who can control and destroy them.

Simply put, to destroy your fears you must fight them by asking yourself, "What's the worst that can happen?" Figure out if there is a solution or a silver lining, and your fears won't scare you anymore!

It's like knowing that you possess the vaccine for a killer virus—even if you catch it, you know how to end it.

In the end, you control your fears, so don't let them control you anymore.

GOLDEN SECRET #36

What is self-sufficiency? Well, it starts with knowledge—of yourself and the world around you. When you are able to stand on your own two feet, so to speak, then you can cut out the bad parts of your life much more easily and help bring in more good parts. Self-sufficiency can start small. Do you live in the city? Learn the bus routes and walk to your nearest grocery store for food if it's close enough. Do you live in the country? Raise chickens or rabbits to help supplement your food supply. No matter where you live, you can also learn to mend your own clothes or learn first aid and CPR just in case of emergency.

One of the most important aspects of self-sufficiency is making your own money. If you are dependent on someone to care for your everyday needs, then what are you going to do if that person becomes a toxic presence in your life or if they leave your life completely? You'll have to start from scratch, and it will be much harder to pull yourself up by your bootstraps than if you were able to provide for yourself the whole time.

Independence is a similarly necessary trait. In a political, territorial sense, *independence* means that the residents and population of a territory—a physical, geographical place—exercise self-government and sovereignty over that territory. In a personal sense, it's the idea that you own your own body and self; it's a sense of individual power that you have over yourself.

The good thing about self-sufficiency and independence is that when you have them, you can rely on yourself and don't need anyone else.

We cannot depend on someone else for everything, no matter who it is, to be successful and happy. We need to provide for ourselves sufficient love, care, happiness, success, and financial power in order to have stable lives.

If you fully rely on someone else to take care of you, make you happy, and give you a good life, then just imagine the day that person is not able to provide for you or isn't in your life anymore at all.

You will lose two things: first, you'll lose all that was coming from that person in the first place. Second, you'll have lost the time you did not take to build yourself up. You will find yourself in a very bad place and starting over is very difficult.

This doesn't mean you can't or shouldn't receive love, care, happiness, and financial support from anybody else. It just means that everything you receive from someone else will and should be in *addition* to what you already have. That way, if it's taken away from you for any reason you will still be able to live your life and go on.

Work on being self-sufficient and independent. Let each person in your life be a welcome *addition* to it, not a necessary part of it.

GOLDEN SECRET #37

We all have expectations—mainly from people who are in our lives such as family members, friends, and life partners.

It's totally normal to expect our life partners to respect us, love us, support us, and be a good parent to our children. It's also fine to expect our best friends to be available to support us when we go through something hard. These are normal, regular expectations—not something I am talking about here.

I am talking about the *extra* expectations.

Have you expected your lover to make you a surprise on a special occasion or your best friend to give you the watch you've talked about for six months for your birthday? What happens if that person does not meet your extra expectations? You feel disappointed and deceived. Disappointment and deception are negative feelings. And negative feelings in your relationships will attract more negative feelings, which will engender more negative situations.

And you *don't* want *that*! Your healthy relationship with those people is worth far more than this special surprise or that watch. Look for what your lover or your best friend do in other areas of your relationship that make you happy. Don't focus on that *extra* expectation nor start thinking that because they did not give you what you expected they don't listen to you, care for you, or love you.

The best thing is actually *not* to have extra expectations at all. It may sound extreme, *but the fewer expectations you have for other people, the happier you will be.*

Be grateful and appreciate the good things your loved ones already offer you. Let those extra things come naturally; don't lose sleep over them.

GOLDEN SECRET #38

A WORD, A BAD SITUATION, OR A DIFFICULT PERSON CAN destroy you or even kill you.

It is not easy. Someone may say something to you that just breaks you inside, or you may have a toxic relationship with someone close to you, or maybe you must endure a very bad, unexpected situation. It's hard. It can ruin you.

How can you avoid being negatively affected?

The answer is: *your reaction* is the key.

First, that is, your mental reaction: how you perceive it and how it makes you feel. You have control over that feeling. Second, your physical reaction will follow if you handled everything well in your mind. You can create a good physical reaction and the impact the situation or person has on you will be diminished.

Yes, you can build yourself up as powerfully as ever, but you will always face negativity in the form of words, nasty behaviours, and bad situations. You *can never* completely avoid feeling bad for those things because the older you get, the more you will experience difficult things in life. It's like a Nintendo Mario Bros game: each level gets harder, but each level you also gain more power and everything before it seems easier to handle.

How can you control your feelings and be an unmoving mountain that no negative words, attacks, or bad situations can penetrate?

You must control yourself. You must focus on your reaction. Your reaction will depend a lot on your self-confidence.

When you are truly self-confident, no situation nor person can knock you off balance or affect your emotions.

In a bad situation, be confident that tomorrow will be better; you know you can survive hard times and change the situation for the good. When you are self-confident, no one on Earth can harm you with their behaviour or words because *you know your value*, you know yourself, and you love yourself.

And guess what? The people who attack you may feel intimidated by your self-valuing attitude!

If you are genuinely self-confident, bullying won't faze you the way it would if you were insecure. The way you react to a bully will shut them down forever and it may actually cause them to see you as a role model. If they see fear and a lack of self-confidence in you, they may *increase* their intimidation tactics. Because they themselves have poor self-confidence, they will feed off your poor reaction. They put you down so they can shine.

Remember: in reality, bullies suffer from low self-confidence. They may actually be hiding something they are afraid of being bullied about.

If you have great self-confidence, everyone who bullies you will be surprised by your reaction because you owned your flaws and showed that you are proud of yourself and you love yourself. Just *imagine* their reactions!

Concerning toxic people who always have a negative comment to make about you and everyone else: before reacting and taking things personally, consider that the problem may be with the other person and not you. Always analyse the person and the words they say, and you will see that most of the time it *has nothing* to do with you!

You have power over situations, people, and words, and it's time to stop letting *them* control and define you and your life. Take back your power!

GOLDEN SECRET #39

Your instincts are your best friend. You may ignore your instincts when they try to inform you about certain things, but you must learn to listen. Your instincts are that little voice inside you, that gut feeling you have each time you meet someone new or decide to do something.

And 100% of the time your instincts are a 100% right!

Your instincts normally make you feel an energy, either positive or negative, and will speak to you in the form of a physical vibration that will become a certain feeling once you have learned more about it.

Intuition and instinct are closely related. Intuition is something you just *know without knowing why*, in a manner of speaking, and instinct is the innate reaction to outside stimuli. For example, an intuitive and instinctual person may pull her child out of harm's way just as a car flies past on the street where the two are walking. She didn't think about doing it or deliberate on whether it was the right thing to do—she just acted and likely saved her child's life. Next time you have "a hunch," just go with it without trying to understand it or instead of ignoring it. You may be surprised by the outcome!

Intuition is the bridge between instinct and conscious reasoning, and it's okay to use all three in order to get further ahead in life. Whether or not "women's intuition" is hardwired or a byproduct of cultural expectations that have to do with gender roles and parenting children, it's important for you to dig into the idea that sometimes you may just know without knowing why, and that's okay. A person's instinct, for example, may tell you to stay at the job you currently have, but your intuition may be telling you to quit your job to start your own business. Compare and contrast your feelings and rational thinking, and if you have a strong gut feeling about starting a new business, you're probably relying on intuition to guide your way. (The main difference between the two is that instinct often relies on fear while intuition relies on unconscious or subconscious knowledge and belief.)

The more you cultivate your spirituality and connect with your soul, the more powerful your instincts will be. It's like developing abilities that will let you read situations and people easily and anticipate things that are going to happen before they happen.

Everyone has instincts, but not everyone listens or believes or trusts them.

Learn to trust your instincts, let them guide you, and you will see improvement in your life's decisions and choices.

GOLDEN SECRET #40

Everything in the world is made from energy, and everything sends out energy.

Energy is sent through a type of vibration, either positive or negative.

Being able to read energy is a special power that you possess within you because it is related to your instincts. All human beings possess it but not all at the same level.

Reading energy is something you can improve by paying special attention to it. The more you tune into the energy that everyone and everything sends, the more you can read it.

You may know it as the term: *a vibe*. And here, I'll give you great advice:

Always trust the energy you feel around people, things, and situations.

The person's vibe (or thing's vibe, or situation's vibe) will indicate to you if it's good or not. And you should take action toward what you genuinely feel.

Energy is something you *feel*, not see. It's like a sixth sense, and you should *always* listen to and trust it. *Energy is free information for you.*

Energy gives you real information about everything and everyone.

The more you listen to it and the more you know how to read it, the more you can use it to make better choices and live a better life.

GOLDEN SECRET #41

What you say will become reality. Believe it or not, it's true. Your words are a weapon that you should use carefully and wisely. Use your words only to spread goodness.

Your thoughts are in your mind, but your spoken words are a materialization of them in real life.

Everything that you think about can become real if you speak it out loud. You send your thoughts into the universe, you create them in the physical world, and you can't remove them once they've been created. You can remove a bad thought from your mind, but it's very hard to remove a bad spoken thing, whether it was spoken to yourself or someone else.

Everything you say has an effect. *Everything*. As we have always heard: *WORDS HAVE POWER.*

So remember, *always think before you speak.*

Choose to say only positive, good things. Evaluate yourself regularly—each day if possible—and ask yourself, "Did I say mostly good or bad things today?" Be aware of your vocabulary and each word that comes out of your mouth.

The more you put good into the world, the more beautiful you and your life will become, and you will attract to you what you materialized with your good words.

Plus, you never know when someone else may need to hear your good words to change their day for the better. You may even change their *life* for the better!

Always, always, always: think before you speak!

GOLDEN SECRET #42

Have you ever lost a very good opportunity you really wanted? Have you ever met someone who was wonderful and you lost the opportunity of having this person in your life? Why did that happen to you?

Because you lacked self-confidence, or you were afraid, or you were too lazy to make an effort.

Let's take those three things individually in turn. First, if you lack self-confidence, you can take heart that by reading this book you will already be working on that! Lacking self-confidence means that you fear criticism from others, have feelings of inferiority, lack assertiveness, are a perfectionist, or some combination of the above! A person who has poor self-confidence may give excuses for their actions or over-compensate in other ways to make up for the fact that they feel low. Of course, everyone wants to be accepted, but fearing criticism will only hinder your personal growth. Similarly, no one is inferior to anyone else! Every human is interesting, creative, and worthy of love from others—and that includes you. I know that just telling you may not change your mind about feeling inferior, but give yourself permission to be great at something. You don't have to be great at everything or even most things, but every person can be great at *some*thing.

Second, let's look at fear. Have you lost an opportunity or a person in your life out of your own fear? (It's okay to admit it —everyone has at some point in their lives.) As Frank Herbert wrote in *Dune*, "Fear is the mind-killer. Fear is the little-death…" Don't let fear bring you a little-death! Push through it and have courage. That's what courage is, after all: it's not the lack of fear. Courage is being afraid and then *doing it anyway*. Give yourself permission to fear if you need to, but also keep in mind that you can do whatever you put your mind to. Don't let it overwhelm you or paralyze you.

Finally, you might have been lazy. Though most missed opportunities are because of the first two reasons, you may just have not wanted to get up off the couch. For this problem, you must find in yourself what motivates you and move toward that thing. You must get to a point in your life that doing *some*thing is less painful than not doing anything.

When that happens, you will overcome your laziness and begin your journey anew!

When opportunity comes into your life, you must jump on it! Put all fears and laziness aside and make the necessary effort to make it happen. If you don't, you may miss the train, and that train may never come down the track again!

Don't let good opportunities slip from your fingers so easily. Go for them, and make them yours!

GOLDEN SECRET #43

NOTHING NEW WILL COME FROM WITHIN YOUR COMFORT zone. No change will come from the same old thing. If you want major positive change in your life, you must challenge yourself and say goodbye to that comfy cosy zone—mentally and physically.

You are stuck in your comfort zone because you are afraid of losing the good things you already have. It's your security, where you feel safe, but nothing great or new will come from it.

Even if you can see your goals as the perfect place you want to be, you may be afraid to make drastic changes because you fear losing what you have now.

But where you are right now is not helping you evolve. It's not helping you grow. It's keeping you from reaching your dreams and achieving your goals. It's keeping you from the best version of yourself and your life. You're stuck with the same results every day.

If you want something different, you have to do things differently. If you want more of the same, keep doing what you're doing now.

Nothing will change if you are not willing to take risks. And actually, you are right to be afraid because there are two sides to taking risks: you either succeed, or you fail.

There is always something to lose in taking risks!

Now even if you fail, what have you really lost? "The effort, the time," you may say, but at least you know that that road was not a good one. There is no doubt that you will find a new way to reach your goal. It will be another risk, and you will risk all over again. Learn from your previous mistakes, and do better each time until you reach the place you want go! It's not that you succeed or fail; it's that you succeed or *learn.*

Dare to risk! Risks are the road to your greatest dreams!

EXERCISE

1. Name a situation in which you regret not taking a risk.
2. Name a way that you can take a risk today that could change your life.

GOLDEN SECRET #44

EVERY SINGLE DAY YOU ARE FACED WITH *PROBLEMS*!

They are in everyone's lives. No human being on this Earth is not faced with problems at every level.

Sometimes, when you encounter a problem, even if it's very small, you may overreact and completely lose your mind and self-control. You may focus on that problem so much that your body and mind begin to experience something called *stress*. When this happens, you have unintentionally married your worst enemy, cortisol (known as the stress hormone)!

You can find out from the internet what cortisol and stress can do to you, so let's keep it simple here. If you experience chronic stress, you may begin to feel overwhelmed by new problems that appear because they add stress on top of the stress you are already feeling. Stress becomes a tree with deep roots inside every part of you, and you make that tree grow by providing the best environment for it.

If stress is at the root of your life's choices, reactions, emotions, and relationships, you must of course find a cure for it.

So, what is the best cure?

You must train yourself to be solution oriented. That is how to destroy a major part of the stress you are living now.

When you become a solution-oriented person, you:

1. Anticipate future problems.
2. Find possible solutions ahead of time.
3. Don't take problems personally. They don't move you or put you in a negative state of mind.
4. Fix problems immediately and quickly move on.

Being solution oriented is a mindset. With this mindset, no problem seems overly complicated nor will you stress out over it anymore. Like a muscle, the more you train this mindset, the stronger it becomes.

Every problem in this world has a solution, and you can find it.

Live with this in mind. Be sure that you have a way to fix any problems that you may come across, no matter what happens to you. And with each problem you face, remember that there are growth benefits for you! By turning problems into opportunities, you will gain self-confidence and kill chronic stress forever!

GOLDEN SECRET #45

SEEING THE GOOD IN BAD SITUATIONS IS A WINNER SKILL FOR a positive mindset!

Let's be honest here: no one is living a fairy tale life. Life is a series of ups and downs for everyone. We all live through good *and* bad situations.

When it's good, everything is beautiful and perfect.

But when it's bad, how do you react? How do you take it?

Most of us will reject it and focus on it in a negative way by complaining and making it even worse.

No matter where you are in life, bad things will happen to you as well as good things. This will be true for your entire life.

To keep yourself safe from amplifying a bad situation and nourishing it with more negativity, you must be able to see the good that comes from it.

You must change your perception of the bad thing so that it becomes an opportunity instead of a burden.

Notice how you see something and how you react to it. You can control the effects of a bad thing by simply changing your perception of it. Avoid reacting immediately if you can. Instead, analyse the bad situation or thing to discover if there may be something positive that comes from it as well. Usually, you can find *some*thing good.

Believe with all your heart that everything happens for a reason. Every bad thing that's happened to you that you wish you could undo is actually part of the reason for a good thing that will happen to you in the future.

Why don't you try to uncover a silver lining? Even if there is nothing positive in what happened to you, you survived it and that in itself is a good thing.

Remember, you succeed, or you *learn*. Every time you survive something negative, it has made you a stronger woman with more experience and knowledge.

And who knows? Maybe one day you will know why it happened.

Learn to see the silver lining in negative things, and you will be invincible: no bad will ever be able to destabilize you!

GOLDEN SECRET #46

Haters, haters, haters. We all complain about them.

Haters are those people who hate on you, especially when you do good things or when you are at your best.

If you do something great or you *are* someone great, there will be someone or some people who shower you with negative comments, start rumours about you, and question everything you do. Then, be sure that you have nothing wrong in you. You are just amazing and that bothers them on a very deep level.

Haters suffer from your being better than them. They suffer so much that they have to react in order to feel relieved from the pain you give them when you shine.

When people hate on you, you can be sure that it's because they are seeing something great in you that they lack.

When they hate on you, they have a clear purpose:

First, they want to diminish you in the eyes of the people who admire you. They may start rumours about you within your entourage. You can't be that perfect, they think, so they invent stories about you to lower your positive effect on the world. (But actually, they will grow your popularity this way because you will get even more attention, so thank them!)

Second, they attack you to destabilize you. Haters want to cause you to respond negatively and show everyone else you are and ugly person!

Third, they put you down to show that what you have is common and not that special. Haters want to bring you down to their level.

A hater's biggest dream is that you disappear from this this solar system because you get all the attention, admiration, and love that they think they deserve but haven't received themselves.

Never take their attitude towards you personally. Stay confident no matter how badly they treat you in person or speak of you behind your back. Haters have trouble with their own selves, trust me, and not you.

Ignore, ignore, *ignore* the haters. Let them hate until the end of the world, but do not reply to their hate by any means. Replying will only give them attention, which is exactly what they seek. Stay focused doing your own thing, enjoying yourself, and living your life.

When you interact with your haters, give them love with a positive attitude and put a smile on your face on top of that. It will destroy them forever!

You must act this way because *you are a good person*. Don't change your personality and your values or become a bad person because of them. They aren't worth it. Don't fight hate with hate. Instead, fight hate with *love*. Haters lack love. When you are a wonderful person and you have love for yourself and your life, you can spare some of your love even for people who may hate you.

So, when haters give you hate, offer them love in return!

GOLDEN SECRET #47

YOU CAN'T CHANGE OTHER PEOPLE, THAT IS A FACT.

Let's pretend you have a friend who believes that money is hard to make and that you have to work until you burn yourself out in order to be a millionaire. On the other side, you already *are* a millionaire and you be- came one easily and quickly because you were convinced money is easy to make. Even if you are both the same age and come from the same place, your back- ground, teaching, knowledge, parents, and life experiences are not the same, and that is why you both have different beliefs.

Now imagine what would happen if you made it your life's purpose to help your friend believe that money is easy to make and keep. You may succeed, or you may not, but in either case, it's going to take you lots of effort and time.

Why must you convince your friend to change his or her beliefs in the first place?

Though we may focus on changing the people around us to make them fit in our lives, the truth is that *people believe only what they want to believe.*

It is already hard to change your own self and believes so imagine trying to change other people's.

It is what is what it is... *you really can't.* If someone is used to cutting his or her sandwich even though you have never cut your sandwich, don't try to make that person eat his or her sandwich like you do.

Accept the differences in other people. When building relationships, be willing to accept that people have their own beliefs and perception of life. Don't try to change them because you will waste your life without success!

Finally, instead of putting forth time and effort trying to change others, put that time and effort into changing *yourself* to be the person you want to become.

GOLDEN SECRET #48

PEOPLE WILL *ALWAYS* TALK. NO MATTER HOW PERFECT YOU are or what good situation you are in. It's human nature, and no one can change it.

When I say *people*, I'm including everyone here, not just haters. The term *people* means even the good ones in your entourage or in society at large.

People always have something to say about something, and I think you probably do, too! We comment upon, judge, and critique everything and everyone.

Of course, the more popular you are or the more successful you are at something, the more people will talk about you: for good or ill.

If you have something special that no one else in your entourage has, you will be noticed more and you will receive more judgement and critique.

Because human beings want to be accepted, we tend to dramatize when people judge, criticize, and talk about us. Sometimes it becomes such a big deal that we are deeply affected. We may start taking everything personally and focus only on what others say about us. We become victims of our own minds and begin questioning ourselves and everything we do.

If this is you, you must stop right now!

Because no matter—I repeat, *no matter*—what you do (good *or* bad), people will always have something to say about it. They will always judge or offer a critique; it's human nature, and the problem is *not* you! Please understand this.

From now on, stop taking personally things that people say. Don't listen to it at all. If you do, you may lose confidence in yourself and put yourself in a negative mood. Even worse, you may start to doubt yourself!

Let people say what they want. Don't change yourself or your life just because they talk; keep living your life as you like, and never stop being yourself.

GOLDEN SECRET #49

Living with revenge in your heart is one of the unhealthiest things you can do for yourself. Revenge is a negative feeling, and the more you think about your revenge, the more you'll attract negativity to yourself!

If you want to get revenge on someone else for something they did to you, you will be the only one hurt in the end. The thing that you are planning in your anger will explode in your face, and the other person may not even be affected by it. Even if she is, you are bound to hurt yourself in the process, too.

Now, you may want to instead show them what for. Maybe you want to prove yourself to that person by losing weight or accomplishing that thing they thought you couldn't do. But is this really worth your time? What will you have to show for that? If you do something good just to seek revenge or prove something, then what you do will be like punishing yourself because your intention is not love. You instead force it on yourself, which is not a good motivation for doing something great.

Instead, let that person suffer forever for doing what he or she did. Believe me, that person will get what he or she deserves without your having to so much as lift a finger.

If you are intent on getting revenge, then here is what you must do: *BE THE BEST VERSION OF YOURSELF!*

Be happy, succesful, powerful, healthy, accomplished and above all forgive them. *This* is your best revenge !

GOLDEN SECRET #50

YOU MAY HAVE MADE SOME MISTAKES IN THE PAST THAT STILL make you feel guilty today. Living with that burden, thinking about it day and night, may give you anxiety and depression, and it's unsustainable to support that guilt the way you have been. Whatever the reason that you feel guilty, you feel that you could have avoided making that mistake in the first place.

In this situation, *you subconsciously punish yourself.* You start hating yourself, and you eventually lose your self-worth and self-respect. And that will kill your self-love.

Okay, so now what? Is there a solution?

The fact you feel guilty for some mistake you made already shows you how great you are! If you were as a bad person as you believe, you would never feel bad for what you did!

It's true that you can't change things, and you can't rewind time to try again. But you are here *now*. You are still alive, and life goes on.

Feeling guilty can have a bad impact on your mental health and result in physical trauma. You don't want that, of course. You must free yourself from feeling so guilty.

> You must *genuinely* forgive yourself.

Accept what you did wrong and learn from your mistakes. If you can correct what you did, then do so. If you can't, then you have lived through a cautionary tale and know not do it again in the future.

If someone did something bad to you:

You may hate that person or want to get revenge against them. You live with these strong emotions, and you remind yourself every single day of the hate you have for that person for what they did to you.

This hate is a negative feeling just like guilt. And the problem with these two is that they remain buried deep in your heart for a long time. They *possess* you; hate and guilt control you and cause negative thoughts and actions in your life and toward yourself and everyone else. It certainly directly affects your mental health.

What is the best response to someone who has hurt you so deeply? As hard it may be, the best response is to forgive them. Yes, really.

Forgiveness frees you from negative emotions and pain you carry inside of you. It is a liberation from your mental prison of hate and guilt, and your life will change for the better.

Anyone who hurt you on purpose will suffer. Life has a way of making sure what goes around comes around. Don't lose yourself for it.

You must forgive yourself and others as much as you can. Yes, it's hard. I'm not saying it's easy. But you must free yourself because you may be hurting yourself without realising it.

GOLDEN SECRET #51

LISTENING WILL HELP YOU A LOT IN YOUR COMMUNICATION with the outside world and your relationships with everyone.

When you listen more than you speak, you will learn. And when you learn and acquire knowledge, you will gain power. You will see things coming, and you will be able to analyse the real meanings hidden behind someone else's spoken words. You will be able to respond better in any situation, and you will also say (more of) the right things because you had time to think before speaking.

Please note: there is a big difference between *hearing* something or someone and *listening to* something or someone. Hearing just means that the words went into your ear and your brain acknowledged that someone was speaking. It's involuntary, accidental, and automatic. Listening involves actively engaging yourself in the words that are being said. It requires focused involvement, conscious effort, and—most of all—*practice*.

In order to practice *listening*, make sure to focus on finding meaning in what you hear. You're paying attention to learn, and you have to be alert and attentive. Don't interrupt the person speaking to you; avoid finishing their sentences or talking over them. Finally, you must ask open-ended questions—who, what, where, when, why, and how. Hint: If you could answer your question with a *yes* or *no*, it is *not* an open-ended question. Think of it this way: a yes/no question is like a true/false question on a test, while an open-ended question requires at least a paragraph to answer—maybe an entire essay! Listening to someone (instead of just hearing them) shows that you care and want to learn more. When a person feels listened to, they are more likely to listen to you in return.

Listening to the universe is similar, but you will learn the more you do it that it's different in some ways from listening to other people. Try it right now. Put this book down for a minute or two, close your eyes, and listen. What do you hear? What do you *really* hear? You'll discover that the world isn't as silent as you thought at first. Maybe you can hear the hum of your refrigerator, or maybe you can hear the crickets chirping outside your window. Take it all in without judging and just *be*.

Not only must you listen to other people, but you must listen to the *universe*. Take a moment—without music, without TV, without phone—and just be silent.

Listen even to the silence, which, of course, is not silent.

Slow down. Stop talking and *listen* to the meaning of the words you hear. Truly listen to the information you receive on a physical and psychic level.

You will find knowledge and answers this way, and they will guide you.

GOLDEN SECRET #52

ONCE IN A WHILE, YOURSELF FROM EVERYONE AND everything close to you. Take a moment with yourself to think and meditate.

Start meditating once a week. Then, you can do it for fifteen minutes once a day. The more you are able to meditate, the more you will be able to control yourself and your life.

This is a moment for you to put everything on pause. To take a break from what is and who are around you to be able to process things and find yourself.

We are so consumed by what we are doing, we sometimes forget where we are going.

We are always in a rush. We are surrounded by life's noise, and we can't hear ourselves anymore. So, we must take the time to retrieve ourselves and be alone with ourselves to think about what is going on in our lives. This will help us see things clearer.

Meditation is often found to be difficult at first, but with practice, you can become more in tune with your inner self and the universe around you. The first thing about meditation that you should know is that it's not something you *do*; it's something you *allow* to happen to you. Don't worry if that seems confusing at first! The second thing you should know about meditation is that *not knowing is the beginning of knowing*. In other words, the more you know, the more you know you *don't* know! There is no person anywhere on this planet who is or was perfect at something the first time they tried it. Or the second time. Or the third time. It takes time and practice. Give yourself a break.

Here are some ground rules for beginning and continuing a good meditation practice. First, find a good teacher. This person doesn't have to be perfect, of course, but at the very least they should spend a lot of time in meditation and be able to direct you past the "sit quietly, close your eyes, and watch your breath" phase. Second, choose a simple meditation technique, like focusing on your breath or a lit candle or running water. Ideally, mediation lasts thirty to sixty minutes, but you can start small. Try meditating for five minutes in the first week, then ten minutes the second week, and then twenty minutes the third week. Finally, remember that meditation's benefits come with practice—they are not immediate. It's like running a marathon, not a sprint. The ultimate goal is self-realisation.

You can go on a walk alone, stand in front of the beach, sit under a tree in a park and watch the sky, or do whatever activity you like that puts you in a meditative state of mind.

Being alone is not only distancing yourself from people but also distancing yourself from what you are doing. Save a little time for yourself wherein you have nothing to do and no one to see. *It's a "me, myself, and I" moment.*

Do this as much as you can so that you never lose yourself.

GOLDEN SECRET #53

THERE HAVE BEEN ENTIRE BOOKS WRITTEN ABOUT THIS alone, but let me reiterate the many benefits of travelling. First, it's good for your health. Travelling can literally help you sleep better, lower your stress hormones and blood pressure, strengthen your immune system, and provide a longer life expectancy. In fact, an annual vacation from regular work can cut your chances of a heart attack *in half*. Yes, really.

Second, travelling regularly (at least a couple of times a year) can provide career benefits as well. People who make time for travel tend to be more open-minded, have better planning and communication skills, and are more adaptable than those people who don't travel. These are all transferrable skills that you can take with you to any job you have, from ditch-digger to brain surgeon.

If you travel with a friend or family, you will create wonderful memories with that person that will last a lifetime. If you travel alone, make sure to keep a journal and take lots of photographs so that you can remember all the great places you've been! If you can't physically travel because of your finances or obligations, become an armchair traveller—spend time in your local library learning as much as you can about other places and eat at authentic restaurants to get in touch with some of the flavours of other parts of the world. You can also look up online how to get a penpal in another country so that you can trade letters and learn more about each other and your countries' customs!

Travelling is one of the most amazing things you can do to treat yourself. It's a new activity, so it will give you a break from your daily routine. It will force you out of your comfort zone into an adventure where you will discover infinite possibilities and learn new things.

Travel disconnects you from your everyday world. You will feel like a new person each time you discover a new place. It cultivates your mind, expands your horizons, and makes you grow on every level.

Travelling is something you should do at least once or twice a year. Invest in it the same way you save for buying a new car or wardrobe. Travel feeds your mind and soul.

Make it a life goal. Even if you are afraid of flying in airplanes or you dislike travel, force yourself to do it at least once a year.

If you are someone who *likes* to travel, make sure you discover new places. Even if you want to go back to the places dearest to your heart, try a new destination at least half the time.

Travelling will enlighten your heart and will help you create new memories. You will meet new people and learn about a new culture and new food. It's one of the best things you can do to treat your mind, body, and soul!

GOLDEN SECRET #54

ROUTINE KILLS YOUR BODY, MIND, AND SOUL. IF IT FEELS like your days repeat themselves over and over, then you are stuck in routine, and you need to break out right now.

Routine is a happiness killer, and it stops you from evolving at every level.

Just think about it. You do the same thing every day of your life: you eat the same food, you meet your friends at the same places, and you go to the same shopping malls. You do exactly the same activities day after day, month after month, and year after year.

It will slowly kill you as a person; it will certainly kill your creativity and time (which you can never get back!), and it keeps you from discovering what life has to offer. Routine puts you in a world where there is no possibility for change and may even lead to serious depression.

You don't have to take an airplane to the Himalayas to break out of your daily routine. Instead, it starts with making small changes in your everyday life. Even changing your house cleaning products, coffee flavour, grocery list, or flower type will have a huge impact on your life.

We stick to the things that make us feel comfortable and that we are used to. Sometimes, we won't even change our toothpaste flavour! We keep buying the same things over and over again.

Changing up the flavour in your food will also have a huge impact on your routine. Try new recipes, discover new ingredients, and eat out at different restaurants. Even drinking your favourite coffee in a new or different cup is a small change you can make often, and that will bring you out of your established patterns.

It really starts there. You must cultivate and nurture your need for change. Act in such a way that you always discover new things and change yourself for the better. It can start with the smallest of actions, as we have seen.

After switching out your coffee cup becomes in itself routine, you must diversify your activities. Start something new each month: a dance or painting class, a sport, or anything new that you have never before done. If you can do it in another neighbourhood not far from your home, then go; that's even better. If you have the time, you will also see a new place!

Meeting new people is also an amazing way to break out from your routine. Even if you don't have time for serious relationships, just be open to meet, chat, and discuss with new people, and it will bring you many benefits.

The key to ending routine is *change*. Change will help you discover new things and evolve on all levels! Dare to change and make your life exciting again!

GOLDEN SECRET #55

THINK OF THIS AS A NEW ROUTINE YOU MUST INCORPORATE IN your life as soon as possible: the "coffee with myself" routine.

This is a moment you take for yourself. Grab a piece of paper or your personal journal, go out to a coffee shop, and have coffee with yourself as you would with a friend.

Don't do this at home; it's really important that you get out of the house and head to a coffee shop, and here is why. You may have coffee at home, it's true, but there are so many distractions that you will end up watching videos on YouTube or cleaning the kitchen or reading emails. The point of this activity is not that you drink a cup of coffee while doing whatever you want. The point is to have a "I'm meeting with a friend" mentality.

But why in a coffee shop? There, you are in an environment where your mind is prepared to relax, discuss, analyse, and think. When you are in a coffee shop you are isolated from all personal distractions except your phone, which—of course—you must turn off during your coffee time.

This coffee time is an important meeting you have with the most important person in your life: *yourself*!

During this time, treat yourself as if you are getting to know someone new. Ask yourself the following questions, and write down the answers so that you can go back in the future and look at how much you've changed—and how much you've stayed the same! You don't need to answer all these questions at one time, so give yourself time and space to really think about your answers and write them down fully.

- Where do I want to be in the next one, five, or ten years?
- If I continue doing what I am doing, where will my life be in one, five, or ten years?
- What is my *why*?
- What am I grateful for?
- What are my values? Am I being true to them?
- Do I worry too much about what others think?
- What do I want people to say about me at my funeral?

- What would I do if I wasn't afraid of anything?
- What would I do if today was my last day?
- Is my social circle positively influencing my life?
- Am I living a lifestyle that promotes physical, mental, and spiritual wellbeing?
- Am I giving enough time to the people who I value the most?
- Do I care more about how my life looks or how it feels? Why?
- If I were to die tomorrow, what would be my biggest regret?

You can, of course, also ask yourself simpler questions, like "What is my favourite colour?" but keep the above questions in mind so that you don't lose sight of your goals and dreams.

It's best to do this at least a couple times a week, as you can. In this special moment, focus on yourself, analyse your situation, fix your goals, review your plans, think about your life, write your thoughts, and enjoy a nice cup of coffee!

This is your private meeting with yourself, so enjoy it and make it entirely yours!

GOLDEN SECRET #56

HAVING A TALK WITH YOURSELF MENTALLY IS GOOD. BUT speaking out loud to yourself in front of a mirror is better! You may think it's crazy, but just do it once, and you will see its amazing benefits.

When you have a problem, you talk about it with someone, right? When you confess to someone, you feel a human presence. Someone listens, feels, and understands you. You both discuss, and she analyses your situation and proposes possible solutions to you.

What if you started doing that with yourself?

No one is able to understand you better than you yourself. The answer to your problem is always inside of you.

Let the first person you speak to about your problems be yourself. That doesn't mean you cannot have support and consolation from someone else, of course. We all need to share our emotions and thoughts with someone we trust who can support us in hard times. But surely you have felt once or twice that no one seems to understand you. In these moments, we feel even more lost because no one else can give us a real solution for what we are going through.

Take some time apart. Get comfortable sitting or standing in front of your mirror. Look at yourself and open your heart as though you were talking to someone in front of you.

By talking to yourself, you will not only bond with yourself but you will begin to understand yourself even more.

You can reveal all your secrets with no shame, open your heart, cry and feel weak without worrying about judgement. It will relieve you from the greatest sorrows and help you solve the biggest problems. You will start consoling yourself, finding solutions, and even negotiating with yourself.

Speaking to yourself in front of a mirror also has other benefits, such as increasing your self-confidence. If you are shy or have difficulty expressing yourself, try speaking in front of a mirror. It will help you be more communicative.

GOLDEN SECRET #57

What's in your heart shows on your face, and you reflect to the world exactly what you have in your heart through the vibes you send into the universe.

Have you ever seen Disney's *Snow White and the Seven Dwarves*? If not, go on YouTube and watch the trailer of the movie. Analyse the physical features of both the Evil Queen and Snow White herself.

If they were both wore exactly the same thing and had the same hairstyle and make up, could you distinguish the Princess from the Evil Queen? Hopefully, your answer is *yes*.

How is that possible if they are both wearing the same clothes, make up and hair?

The answer is this: *What's in someone's heart shows in their face and throughout their being.*

The Evil Queen is a very beautiful woman. Look at her facial features; they are beautiful. But when we see her face, we know she is not a good person. Her beauty can't mask her heart full of hate, jealousy, envy, and revenge.

What is in her heart shows on her face, and we naturally read faces and make psychological notes in our subconscious mind when we see someone face for the first time. We don't even need the person to speak or act because we can tell that she is a good (or bad) person just by reading her facial expression.

Remember, physical beauty and style cannot make you appear beautiful if you have a heart full of hate, revenge, and negativity. You will attract people and situations to your life equal to what is in your heart. No matter how much you wear beautiful, expensive clothes and exquisitely groom yourself, nothing will be able to hide what's in your heart. We don't judge others just with our eyes only; we judge others with our feelings, exactly the way you can tell who is the Evil Queen and who is the innocent Princess.

When you hold onto negative emotions, your face and body will react accordingly. Let's say you are at an event and someone you hate sits next you. Imagine how your facial expression and body language will look when you react to that feeling of hate. Your emotion will be obvious to anyone who sees you in that moment because they saw it in your face and body language.

Do this experiment right now with if you have a mirror or with the camera of your cell phone. Look at yourself and think about something that makes you angry. Watch how your facial expression makes you ugly even if you are beautiful. Now, think about someone you love, and watch how your expression changes.

Even though you attend an event wearing the most beautiful outfit with the most beautiful grooming, if you feel hate or other negative emotions, you will significantly decrease your perceived beauty.

The opposite is also true. You can be in the worst physical state ever, but if you feel positive emotions, then your beauty will increase.

Beauty is not about the perfection of your facial features, body shape, clothes, or accomplishments. It's about what's in your heart. The better a person you are, the more beautiful your heart is and the more others will find you beautiful as well.

So, fill your heart with good and unleash your true beauty!

GOLDEN SECRET #58

A GENUINE SMILE THAT COMES FROM YOUR HEART IS A SIGN of happiness. If you don't smile much, it may mean there is something wrong inside of you.

Your smile is a tool you can use to measure your emotional health.

A genuine smile comes from positive emotions. The more positive you are and the more you enjoy life, the more you'll smile.

If you don't smile enough, the best way to rectify the issue is to consciously smile—fake it until you make it. Smiling is contagious. When your body feels that happy reaction, it will want more of it. So, if you are in a bad stage of life and you lost that spark of joy, make a conscious effort to have fun, watch funny things, be with funny people, and put your smile

A smile is the best accessory you can own, the best make up, the best outfit and the best physical attribute you possess. When you smile from your heart, your eyes will shine and your face will light up. This is *not* the Crest smile where you show your teeth without emotion.

Be funny, have fun, and don't take life too seriously! No life is perfect, and you may have a lot to deal with, but never lose your smile. It will enlighten your life, your heart, and your face! Don't let anyone bring you down.

GOLDEN SECRET #59

Always be proud of yourself, no matter what!

When you reach a goal—even a small one—take the time to enjoy your victory. Congratulate yourself on whatever good you do for yourself or others. There's no action too small! Opening the door for an old lady at the mall or letting a pregnant woman take your seat on the bus still count.

We sometimes do great things and we think it's normal and no big deal. But actually, we are amazing and good achievements prove how great we are.

Thank yourself for what you did and feel proud of it. Be proud of yourself, treat yourself, and gift yourself as if you were dealing with someone you cherish.

Because, in fact, you love yourself!

GOLDEN SECRET #60

It will benefit you to maintain a positivity journal where you can write your goals and dreams or even whatever is on your mind that's good.

This is a place where you put your good thoughts out into the physical world and where you describe your goals and dreams. It's the place where you write your plans in order to transform them into real life action.

Writing your goals, dreams, and good plans actually helps to make them happen. When you put them into the physical world, they're not just bouncing around in your head anymore.

If you don't maintain a journal now, I strongly suggest you start one that you consult daily. Write in it as much as possible. Write about what you have on your mind: your ideas, your wishes, and all the positive things you want in your life.

Here are some ideas of what to write about in your positivity journal:

- Things that always put you in a good mood.
- What your perfect day would look like.
- A gratitude list of things you're thankful for.
- Your favourite thing about yourself.
- A list of positive "I am…" statements.
- What you do to make yourself feel better when you're down.
- What inspires you.

Remember, this is a *positivity* journal! Don't write about your annoying coworker, the fight you just had with your parents or partner, or the bill you forgot to pay that was buried under a stack of other paperwork. *Do* write about the promotion you just got at work, the flowers your partner brought home for you just because, or the money you found in your coat pocket last week when you thought you didn't have any cash!

In addition to writing in your positivity journal, think about one thing you can do today to help make your dreams and goals a reality. For example, if you want to be a doctor, you can make sure to study human anatomy and memorize all the parts of the body. If you want to be a caring mother, you can spend a little more time with your children or promise yourself you'll be more patient with them today than you were yesterday. Write down what you're going to do today in your journal to help make sure that you stick to your mini-goal! When you do this every day, you will make progress to your goals and dreams.

This is *not* a journal where you write your problems or life story. It's strictly a "no negativity" zone. *Your journal should inspire you each time you open it.*

You must also make a habit of consulting it twice daily: when you wake up in the morning and before you go to sleep. It will help you stay inspired and motivated, and you won't forget your goals or plans and actions to achieve said goals.

GOLDEN SECRET #61

Where do we find motivation when we want to achieve a dream or goal?

You know that feeling: you want to achieve something, but it feels like something is holding you back. Have you ever experienced one of these situations?

You clean out your fridge and buy healthy foods at the grocery store. You get rid of all the junk food in your house, but you never start the meal prep you intended to start.

Or, you begin a gym membership and make yourself a workout plan. You even buy yourself the most amazing training outfit, but you end up going the first time and then you stop.

And eventually you feel guilty for quitting (or never starting) and you decide to start tomorrow. But tomorrow comes, and you never start.

Why does this happen? The answer is this: it is a lack of motivation because your goal was not *vital* to you.

The external motivation you had to *start* something was not powerful enough to give you the desire to continue. In order to be truly *internally* motivated, you need to crave your dream or goal so much that you can't *not* do it.

For example: for a growing baby, walking is *vital*. He *must* do it in order to survive. That is why his motivation is so solid. *If you don't see your goal as something vital in your life, it will not motivate you enough to persevere and reach it.*

Keep up, work hard, and *never* stop. And when the little voice in the back of your mind gives you a million reasons to be lazy or to quit, shut it down and remind yourself how vital your goal is. You can control it!

If you lack motivation for a very big goal, then try dividing it into smaller, more accomplishable goals and pursue *those* goals until you reach your final destination.

If you are still stuck and don't have sufficient motivation, then: *start*. Complete a small, tiny, simple step. This small action toward your goal will motivate you to take a second step because you are getting results.

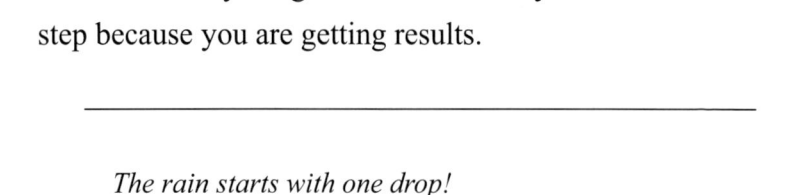

The rain starts with one drop!

Motivation has a snowball effect: when you work toward your goal and see results—even if they are small—your motivation grows.

Motivation is like the fuel for a vehicle: without it you can't even start! There *will* be ups and downs in your motivation, but always remember why you started. Remember what you want to accomplish, and your motivation will grow!

Motivation, perseverance, and consistency are the keys to achieve anything you want in life. If you want something to happen, if you want to reach your goals, you must possess those three things.

Temptation and distractions will always be there to distract you and to keep you from reaching your goals and dreams. It takes a lot of self-control and self-discipline not to be affected.

If you arm yourself with perseverance and consistency, nothing will be able to stop you.

Remember the baby from earlier? He walks on his feet and falls again and again and again, but because walking is *vital* for him, he will not stop until he stands on his feet and runs! The baby is *persevering*: working harder and harder even after falling, and he does it *consistently* every single day until he reaches his goal.

Now if you are already motivated but you're stuck, the best thing to do is start slowly. Grow your effort with time. Don't be hard on yourself at the beginning. Go slowly but surely.

Don't rush things. Everything is a process.

So, whether your goal is big or small, make a plan. Write out the goal, the schedule, and the actions you will take. Split your efforts and gradually work toward your goal in the time you gave yourself. And most importantly, follow your plan.

For example: you want to participate in a five-hour marathon but you can't even run for five minutes. If the marathon is next year, start *today*. Create for yourself a plan where you run for ten minutes every day for the first two weeks, then twenty minutes a day for three weeks, then forty minutes a day for six weeks and so on.

There is a Japanese method that teaches us to do something for one minute every day, no matter what your goal is. Begin by doing the action for one minute each day, and gradually and naturally you will put more time into it because you will be used to it and not want to stop.

Remember: perseverance and consistency are your best the best tools to reach your goals !

GOLDEN SECRET #62

IT IS *IMPOSSIBLE* FOR YOU TO REACH SUCCESS IF YOU AVOID defeat, making mistakes, and handling hard times.

It's one of the laws of the universe. (If no one told you that before, then now you know!)

Success is a process. That is why it never happens overnight.

No *real* success ever comes to you the first time. You must face difficulty and defeat repeatedly, and you will also make numerous mistakes. It's the only way to get to real success. Do not look at defeat as something that will hold you back. Don't let mistakes stop you. Remember, you succeed, or you *learn*.

No baby came to this life without his mother struggling during labour and delivery.

Every champion athlete passes through defeat to win a gold medal at the Olympics.

Each successful entrepreneur made many mistakes before becoming a multi-millionaire.

Do not let the hard moments bring you down. The mistakes and defeat that comes to your way will help you savour your victory when it eventually comes.

Remember this: success is a process, not an event. Believing that success is an *event* means that you think the good outcome can be traced back to one thing, like winning the lottery or inheriting a lot of money from a long lost relative. Believing that success is a *process* is knowing that the outcome comes from incremental change and cumulative effort. Someone once said, "It takes fifteen years to be an overnight success," and they were right! Every overnight success story you've heard has a backstory that includes a lot of hard work and patience. The only way to truly fail at something is to give up. If you are defeated one day, get up the next morning and try again.

It's okay to go through the hard moments and sit with the pain and sorrow for a little while, but don't let those feelings distract you from your goals and dreams. You know you are getting closer to achieving them *because* you are going through hardship. If you are going through hell, *keep going.*

Making mistakes is one way you know you're growing and learning; it is the rich soil and water that produces the blooming flower that is your goal. Or, to put it another way, defeat and mistakes are the refiner's fire; they create the pure gold that you want to become.

Luck is what happens with preparation meets opportunity. When you are working toward your goals and dreams, you are making yourself prepared for whatever comes your way, despite the defeat you endure, the mistakes you make, and the hardship you overcome. So always be prepared and you will invite good luck into your life.

GOLDEN SECRET #63

If you have a goal or a dream, go for it and never quit!

Creating goals for yourself is a way for you to grow and improve yourself. Each time you decide on a new goal, your subconscious mind makes a way for you to be a better version of yourself.

When you challenge yourself, you make yourself better every time you succeed or learn.

Sometimes we create goals, make resolutions, and strive for a change, but we don't *act*. The goal or dream just remains in our minds and never materializes. In this case, our goals become simply wishes and not goals.

If you don't work toward your goal, no one else will!

Even if you dream and wish and plan, you must still *act*. If you want to improve yourself and your life, you must act for yourself—no one will act in your place. You may start small, but you have to *start*.

Even if your goals seem impossible, keep in mind that if you were able to think it, desire it, and dream it, then your goal is *possible*. I assure you: you are not crazy.

Create a plan for yourself, visualize it, work for it, persevere, arm yourself with courage and patience, and never quit. Make your dreams and goals come to life!

Never let yourself or anyone else cause you to give up on your goals; they are your desires and dreams. They will make you the best version of yourself!

GOLDEN SECRET #64

WITHOUT SELF-DISCIPLINE, YOU CAN'T REACH ANYTHING IN life.

Imagine a famous football player waking up one morning and saying to himself, "Well this morning I won't train. I will procrastinate at home eating chips and chocolate and watching TV instead. I will go tomorrow."

Would he still be a famous professional football player ? You guessed it: *no*.

You need self-discipline to beat that evil voice in the back of your head that is holding you back from success.

From starting a sleep routine to achieving the biggest things in life, you must have self-discipline… or say goodbye to your dreams.

Strengthen your will power and arm yourself with the greatest single key for achievement: *self-discipline*.

Like with many other things, I'm not saying self-discipline is easy, but it's *important*. If you're struggling with self-discipline, you can do several things to help mitigate that. First, know your weaknesses. For example, if you're trying to eat healthier, admit to yourself that chips and chocolate cake are your downfalls! The first step is always admitting you have a problem. Second, remove the temptations. Again, if you're trying to eat healthier, stop buying chips and stop making chocolate cake for yourself! You can't eat it if you don't have it, after all. There's something to be said for the maxim *Out of sight, out of mind*.

It's simple and may seem silly, but you are far more likely to succeed if you remove the temptation from your field of vision, from your sphere of influence so that it can't affect you anymore!

Third, set clear goals and have a plan. If you're trying to eat healthier, for example, what does that mean to you? Does it mean more fruits and vegetables in your diet? Does it mean cutting out soda and cookies? Don't let "eat healthier" get in the way of actually achieving your goal! Fourth, create new habits by keeping it simple. Incremental change adds up to great change in the long run, and that's what we want here for you as well. If you want to start exercising more, don't worry if you're not a marathon runner on the first day! Just work out or take a run for ten or fifteen minutes on the first day, and build up your momentum until you have an exercise practice that you can be proud of.

Finally, change your perception about willpower. Science has discovered that the amount of willpower a person has is directly determined by their beliefs. In other words, if you *believe* you have all the willpower in the world, you *do*. And visa versa, if you place a limit on your willpower, you will probably reach that limit before you reach your goals.

GOLDEN SECRET #65

SOMETIMES, IT'S EASY TO HATE WHEN SOMEONE GIVES US advice on something we are doing. Even our own parents did it! Remember when they chided you when you were a child? "At your age I didn't eat junk food the way you do today. You should eat less junk food; it'll make you sick!" It's so easy to take this as an *attack*!

You become defensive, and you decide not to care about what they told you. You may even do the reverse of what they told you just to spite them.

Of course, a person's tone—the *way* something is said—can impact us a lot. Someone may try to give us advice but they just don't have the right tone, and we ending up taking it as an attack or critique.

In life, two of the best things that can prevent you from making mistakes and can guide you more quickly to a goal or a desire is, first, learning from others' experiences and, second, accepting genuine advice.

If someone wanted had the same goal as you, then they took that road before you, and, whether or not that person succeeded, they know more about it than you. This is called *experience*.

A famous person once said, "Learn from the mistakes of others. You can't live long enough to make them all yourself." It's true that we remember people's failures more than their successes, and if we can learn from those failures, we will not have to make them ourselves! If someone gives you advice and they didn't say it very nicely, try to see past the wrapping and get to the core of the advice. If your father says, "You should eat less fast food!" what he really means is "I'm concerned about your health. I would like you to take better care of yourself." When you reframe the advice given to you that way, you can see that the delivery is not the core message.

You want to be in the group of people who learns from your own experience *and* the experiences of other people. For example, let's say you are walking on the sidewalk and you see someone ahead of you trip over a tree root that's sticking out of the pavement. If you are paying attention, you know instinctively to be more aware of the tree root when you get to that spot in the sidewalk so you don't *also* trip. You should do this in every part of your life, not just when you are trying to avoid tripping! Being aware of what is around you is one way to help defend against avoidable injury—whether that be injury to your person, your family, or your work.

Learn from others' experiences because it is free, valuable information for you that may provide you shortcuts in order to reach your goals.

Be willing to accept genuine advice, and *ask* for it in whatever you do. Most of the time, it will guide you well.

GOLDEN SECRET #66

Constructive criticism may be hard to hear, but it will help you grow and evolve. You may work in the public sector and already receive constructive criticism on a daily basis, or you may be critiqued at work or within your family or in your entourage.

When we get critiqued, we may react negatively at first. We tend to think people are attacking us and may even see the criticism as insulting. But we must differentiate truly constructive feedback from the negative, hurtful comments.

A useful critique will come from someone who loves and appreciates you. Genuinely helpful feedback helps you improve something in yourself, and it is not intended to offend or to diminish you. It's really important to understand the difference between this and hurtful comments.

If you have already received a critique that you think was made with good intent, accept it. Take it as a statement of love and see if the advice can make you better at something.

If you have never received constructive criticism, ask someone you love and trust to critique you. It may sound strange, but it will feed you in a way you have never before known!

Ask this person how they see you. Ask them to tell you the top five best and top five worst things about you.

For example, a genuine critique could include:

- You are too impulsive.
- You neglect yourself physically.
- You take things too personally.
- You respond to negative statements with bad words.
- You have bad eating habits.
- You give too much to people who don't deserve it.

Usually, we see ourselves only from our own perspectives, and we behave accordingly. When someone who cares about you gives you constructive feedback, their perspective and analysis could help you a lot. After all, they see things you cannot see in yourself, and they can therefore help you improve and evolve.

Make sure this person is someone who truly loves and cares about you and is trustworthy. If you can ask three to five people, it would be even more helpful because you'll receive different points of view.

Don't be scared of honest critique; it is a key to creating the best version of yourself!

GOLDEN SECRET # 67

WHATEVER BAD SITUATION YOU ARE IN RIGHT KNOW, whatever struggle you may be enduring at this very moment, whatever dark place you are in mentally or emotionally, remember to *hope*. Even if you feel that there is no light ahead of you and no possible happy ending: *never lose hope*.

Never lose hope in yourself and in life. You have no idea how the situation can still change!

It may seem like there is no tomorrow or there is no possible way to be happy again. Maybe you cannot imagine any possible solutions to your problem, but you don't know what tomorrow has to offer you. No one can predict the future!

Even if you are in the worst place ever at this very moment, keep in mind: nothing is forever. You will not suffer forever. Time heals all wounds. Things change; there is always something better waiting for you.

You must just allow time to work its magic. Be patient, be grateful, and be positive.

That doesn't mean stay there, sitting, not doing anything, and waiting for miracles. You must also *act*. Believing in a better future, and act accordingly. Even a baby step is still a step.

There is always light in the darkness, and the proof is when the night comes you can still see the world. The Moon and stars provide light.

Even if you are at the lowest point in your life that you have ever been, don't give up! *Hope* is the internal belief that things can get better—and that eventually, they will. If you give up hope of a better day tomorrow, you will become hopeless, which means that you will fall into despair and be overwhelmed by your situation without any way to change it. But you can change it! I promise. Even if you can't change the literal, physical aspect of your low point, you can change how you think about it. Your mind and belief in yourself are things that no one but you have control over—no one can take it away from you. Even if you have no idea how the situation can turn for the better, have hope that it can.

Identify the challenges in your life and situation. You might find that your problem could be influenced by three important factors, which are all influenced by hope. First, you can always change your attitude if it's low. Second, you can increase your effort based on your changed attitude. And third, with your increased effort and changed attitude, you can grow your self-confidence and improvement strategy. Even small steps are still steps, and small steps can still lead to your walking a thousand miles if you want to. When you really dig deep into your goals and dreams, you can make even the tiniest step today, and if you make a tiny step tomorrow, too, you'll be two steps closer than you were! Build on small successes and believe in yourself.

No matter the dark place you are in right now, there is hope. Just look back at a very bad situation that you've already lived through. Things changed, and hopefully you are in a better place now. To help yourself, listen to another person's story of trial and success. This will show you that you are not alone and have something to feel hopeful for!

Never lose faith because you never know what the future has in store!

GOLDEN SECRET #68

PATIENCE IS THE KEY TO EVERYTHING IN LIFE.

Right now, either you are in a good or a bad situation, and either way, having patience will help you get through—even the hardest moments. If you want to achieve something in life, patience is the tool that will lead you there. If you want to resolve a big problem, patience is your key. If you want to heal from an injury, then patience is your solution.

Be patient and watch miracles happen.

Being impulsive and wanting everything to happen immediately will not help you, and it may actually make things worse in some situations where you need to sit back and think before acting.

If you are too impulsive when facing problems, you might do something that could make the problem worse. Arm yourself with patience or the problem may become even harder to solve.

Everything in life is like a baby in his mother's womb. He needs nine months in the womb to come to this life. A mother can't ask for her baby to be born after just one month. She needs to be patient and wait because it's a process.

Did you know that patient people have better mental health? Science has shown that those who are more patient tend to also be more hopeful and more satisfied with their lives. Plus, you'll be happy to know that patience is a skill you can practice—it's not necessarily something you're born with. Even if your life is the best it can be, being patient means that you are empathetic enough to assume personal discomfort in order to lessen the pain and suffering of the people around you. Additionally, patient people are more likely to be better friends and neighbours.

If you're worried that you're not patient enough, try these three things. First, reframe the situation. As I mentioned before, even if you can't change anything about your problem or situation, you can still change your *mind*. Second, practice mindfulness. Notice what you're feeling when you're feeling it by taking a step back from the problem before you start yelling or break down and cry. It can help to take a deep breath and slowly count to ten, for example.

Third, practice gratitude. Be thankful for the things you do have rather than griping about what you don't have. But still make sure to work toward your goals and dreams because without them, you'll patiently go nowhere! If you are patient in everyday situations, though—like when your child asks for a third glass of milk after spilling the first two glasses all over the table—your life will be more pleasant overall and it might even help you find a more satisfying and successful future.

If you act too quickly you may burn bridges and jump over essential steps toward progress. In some cases, you can't backtrack; you have to start all over again from the very beginning.

For everything, we need time. For everything, we must allow enough time to pass to see good results.

La patience c'est la sagesse, or *patience is wisdom*.

GOLDEN SECRET #69

YOUR BEST PARTNER IN LIFE IS NONE OTHER THAN *YOURSELF*!

Yourself is; your healthy, mind, body and soul. Everything and everyone is transient, so *you* are the one and only partner guaranteed to always stay with you. And you are the only person you can change into someone of your dreams.

Be willing to invest in yourself in order to shape yourself to a person you love. Self-love is the root of self-confidence, self-esteem, self-respect and self-value.

The most powerful relationship you can have with a human being in this life is with none other than yourself.

Always keep this in mind and meditate on it. Ask yourself often how much you love yourself— not in a narcissistic kind of way but a true self-love kind of way.

By loving yourself first, you are more likely to care for yourself, and each one of your actions will be with that love in mind. Make that love grow and flourish, listen to it, and take care of it because it'll keep you happy forever!

AFTERWORD

Your healthy, successful, and happy self is your biggest accomplishment and best investment in this life. And to succeed in that, you need *self-love*.

Forget everything else and start loving and working on yourself from this day forward. When you begin to see the fruit of your own self-love, you will become happy and satisfied. When you learn to connect with your deepest self, life will become beautiful! When you value, nurture, care, protect, beautify, fulfil, and respect yourself, you will taste genuine happiness that lasts forever.

Your biggest battle in this life is with yourself, not with anyone or anything else. It is an ongoing struggle, but if you win, then you will access to your best life and the best version of yourself.

You control yourself and everything in your life; this has been purposely repeated to you several times in this book. Never lose that control. It's these words that you must imprint on your mind forever. I even want you to go write them on your walls at home!

I control myself, and I am the only person who does!

Seriously, write those words on a piece of paper and stick it on your bedside table or in any place where you will see it several times a day.

Similarly, write another note to yourself: *I love myself!*

These two affirmations will change your life. Repeat them in your mind and out loud in front of a mirror daily in the morning and before you go to sleep.

Believe and *feel* these words in your heart in order to live by them.

Don't lose any more time in your wild and precious life! Start using the 69 golden secrets you have read in this book and reread if necessary. These golden secrets will guide you to become the best version of yourself.

If you are self-absorbed or consumed by the everyday, reread this guide. If you wake up on any given day feeling low, reread this guide. If you don't have time to read it all over again, then open this book and read only the titles. It will remind you and keep you self-aware. It will give you a boost of motivation so you never lose track of your goals and dreams in life.

Never forget that you are a wonderful, amazing, unique, and special being, and you deserve the best life ever—one filled with love, health, joy, success, satisfaction, and happiness.

LOVE YOUrself!

Angel Gaudia